JESUS —
TO ETERNITY & BEYOND!

JOHN 17-21

KAY ARTHUR
JANNA ARNDT

HARVEST HOUSE PUBLISHERS
Eugene, Oregon 97402

Illustrations by Steve Bjorkman

Cover by Left Coast Design, Portland, Oregon

Discover 4 Yourself Bible Studies for Kids
jESUS—TO ETERNiTY ANd BEYONd!

Copyright © 2001 by Precept Ministries International
Published by Harvest House Publishers
Eugene, Oregon 97402

ISBN 0-7369-0546-4

Printed in the United States of America.

01 02 03 04 05 06 07 / RDP-BG / 10 9 8 7 6 5 4 3 2 1

To my Proverbs 31 mom, Ramona Vickery, who has worked with delight to take care of her family and whose hands have never been idle. And to my daddy, Leon Vickery, who always found time to play with us, for his stories and his imagination, but most importantly for teaching me about Jesus and leading me into a relationship with Him, as well as teaching other children in Sunday school for 35 years. My sister, Rhonda, and I are blessed to have parents who love the Lord and who have given us such priceless gifts of love: a godly heritage, their time, and devotion that we are passing on to our children.

I love you both.

Janna
Deuteronomy 6:1-9

CONTENTS

A Bible Study *You* Can Do!

A BIBLE STUDY YOU CAN DO!

Come on!" The casting call is out for the new movie *Jesus—To Eternity and Beyond!* You did such an awesome job working on our last two movies (*Jesus in the Spotlight* and *Jesus—Awesome Power, Awesome Love*) that we couldn't wait to have you join our crew one more time to film the spectacular finale to Jesus' life.

This will be sooooo exciting working on the film that will show Jesus' last hours before He was crucified. You'll get to capture the disciples' heartbreak and fear, as all seems lost. But then you will film the most stunning scene of all as Jesus shows us He is the Overcomer, the conquering King!

Are you ready to get started? In order to make this movie you will need God's Word and His Spirit to direct and guide you, along with this book. This book is called an inductive Bible study. That word *inductive* means that you will study the Gospel of John and discover *for yourself* what it means. Instead of someone else telling you what the book is about, you'll look at the Bible passages and figure it out for yourself. Isn't that exciting?

There's no time to lose. The director is calling us to the set. We are ready to capture the most suspenseful, heartbreaking, and joyous moments in all of history! Grab those scripts, and let's go!

THINGS YOU'LL NEED ▼

NEW AMERICAN STANDARD BIBLE (UPDATED EDITION)— OR PREFERABLY, THE NEW INDUCTIVE STUDY BIBLE (NISB)
PEN OR PENCIL
COLORED PENCILS
INDEX CARDS
A DICTIONARY
THIS WORKBOOK

1

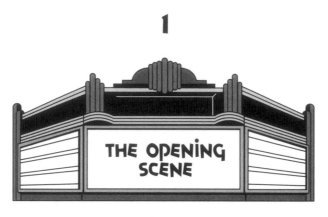

THE OPENING SCENE

JOHN 17

Hey, here we are! Over here! Now that we are back on the set, we need to plan how to shoot our opening scene. The director and the crew are ready for us to take a look at how *Jesus—Awesome Power, Awesome Love* ended so that we can make a smooth transition in our new movie. We don't want our audience to miss one exciting moment in this powerful book of John, so we need to make sure they know what has been happening and where we are as our first scene is captured on film. Let's do a quick review to help our director as he gets the crew ready to go.

DAY 1

LET'S REVIEW THE SCENE

Before we begin our review, there's one more thing we need to do. Pray! We need to get our directions from the Master Director, God. Without Him this would be just another movie. We need to ask God to help us search out truth so that we can understand His script (the Bible). That's why the very first thing we need to do each day as we walk onto the set is pray. Let's do that right now, and then we'll be ready to begin.

WHY did the apostle John write the Gospel of John? Let's see if you can remember the first memory verse you learned in *Jesus—Awesome Power, Awesome Love* that tells us WHY John wrote the book. Our prompter has a cue card below to help trigger your memory. But she has also mixed up the order of the words in this verse just to see how much you remember. Look at the cue card. See if you can put this verse in the right order by putting the right word in the right blank below the cue card. Strike out each word as you use it. This verse from John 20 tells us WHY John wrote this very important book and WHY we're making a movie out of it.

written	Christ	believe	name	believing	Jesus	But	so
you	that	the	have	these	may	of	in
life	been	may	that	His	God	is	and
the	that	have	Son	you			

_____ _____ _____ _____ _____

_____ _____ _____ _____ _____

_____ _____ _____ _____ _____,

_____ _____ ____ _____; _____ _____

_____ _____ _____ _____ _____

_____ _____ _____.

John 20: _____

Now that we know why this book was written, we need to know what has been happening. John 17 is our first scene in our new movie. We need to know WHERE Jesus is and WHO He is with. Looking for WHERE Jesus is will help us discover the *context* of John 17.

When you study the Bible, it is very important to understand the context of a passage. What is context? Context is the setting in which something is told or found. In order to begin the production of our movie, we need to know the setting of John 17. When you look for context in the Bible, you look at the verses that surround the passage you are studying (like reviewing John 16). Then you think about where the passage fits in the big picture of the Bible.

Context also includes:

- the place something happens. (This is geographical context, such as it happening in Jerusalem instead of Los Angeles.)

- the time in history an event happens. (This is historical context, such as the time before Jesus' birth, during His life, or after His death and resurrection.)

- the customs of a group of people. (This is cultural context, such as girls in Bible times did not wear blue jeans, and when people ate dinner they reclined on a couch rather than sitting at a table.)

Sometimes you can discover all these things from just the verses you're studying. But sometimes you have to study other passages of Scripture. It's always important to be on the lookout for context because it helps you discover what the Bible is saying. If you have done *How to Study Your Bible for Kids!* you probably remember all of this.

Now that we know what context is, let's take a look at what has been taking place as John 17 opens up. Let's quickly review what was happening as *Jesus—Awesome Power, Awesome Love* ended.

In our last scenes we saw that Jesus knows His hour has come. Jesus has just had the last supper with His disciples, and Judas has left (John 13). After that, in the next three chapters (John 14–16) we see Jesus having a private conversation with His 11 disciples. He is teaching them to love one another, preparing them for His going away, and comforting them, telling them that He will never leave them alone. He will send the Helper, the Holy Spirit, to be with them always. His last words as John 16 closes remind the 11 disciples that they will face tribulation in the world, but to take courage for He has overcome the world. What awesome love and power!

Now we have the context of where we are as John 17 unfolds. We know the setting: Jesus is with His 11 disciples spending His last hours with them as He prepares them for what is to come.

We need you to create our storyboard for John 17. A storyboard is a sketch of each main scene in a movie. To do your sketch, turn to page 127 in your workbook to your Observation Worksheets. This is where you will study the script and do your research. Read John 17 and then draw a picture in the box below that shows the main event—the main thing that is happening in this chapter. WHAT is Jesus doing? When you finish, write a title on the line below the box. A title is a very brief description that tells what the main event is.

A title should:

1. Be as short as possible

2. Describe the main thing the chapter is about

3. If possible, use words you find in the chapter instead of your own words

4. Be easy to remember

5. Be different from the other titles so that you can tell them apart

John 17

Now that your storyboard is finished, it's time to learn your lines. It is very important to know your script (God's Word). Actors and actresses can't play their part if they don't have their script memorized. One helpful way to learn your lines is to write them down on an index card and read them aloud three times in a row. Do this three times a day: morning, noon, and at night just before you go to bed. Once you have your lines down pat, you will be ready for any scene that God puts you in. So practice your part, and we'll meet you back at the set tomorrow.

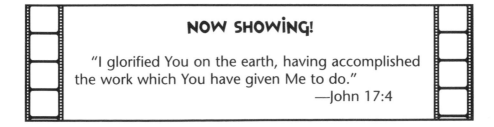

NOW SHOWING!

"I glorified You on the earth, having accomplished the work which You have given Me to do."
—John 17:4

SCAN THE SCRIPT!

We're ready for our second day on the set. How should we begin? That's right! We need to start with prayer, and then we're ready to meet with our screenwriter. The screenwriter needs your help going over the screenplay (the script for our movie). He needs you to find the *key words* in John 17.

What are key words? Key words are words that pop up more than once. They are called key words because they unlock the meaning of the chapter or book that you are studying and give you clues about what is most important in a passage of Scripture.

✸ Key words are usually used over and over again.

✸ Key words are important.

✸ Key words are used by the writer for a reason.

Once you discover a key word, you need to mark it in a special way using a special color or symbol so that you can immediately spot it in Scripture. You also need to watch and see if there are any pronouns or synonyms that go with the key word and mark them also. What are pronouns and synonyms? Take a look at your cue cards below.

PRONOUNS

Pronouns are words that take the place of nouns. A noun is a person, place, or thing. A pronoun stands in for a noun. Here's an example: "The director makes sure everyone is ready on the set. He yells, 'Quiet down!' when he is ready to shoot the first scene." The word *he* is a pronoun because it takes the place of the noun *director* in the second sentence. It is another word we use to refer to the director.

Watch for these other pronouns when you are marking people:

I	you	he	she	me	yours	him
her	mine	his	hers	we	it	our
its	they	them				

SYNONYMS

Synonyms are different words that mean the same thing.

For an example, *sailboat, yacht,* and *rowboat* are different words, but they are all names for kinds of boats. That's a synonym.

Pronouns and synonyms may seem hard, but you can do it! Just keep your eyes open.

Now you're ready to get to work. Turn to page 127 to our Observation Worksheet on John 17. Help our screenwriter by marking the following key words:

glorify

world

love (red heart)

sanctify (color it red and box it in yellow)

hour (mark anything that tells you WHEN with a clock)

whom You gave Me (17:2,6,9—underline it in blue)

hate (make a black heart with a line through it)

one (unity, being one, sticking together with the same purpose and goal—mark it with a 1 and color it yellow)

As you leave the set today, don't forget to "run your lines." Practice makes a great performance. By the way, do you see a key word in your memory verse? Mark it on your index card so that it stands out.

See you tomorrow!

CHECK THE DIALOGUE

A script clerk is in charge of many different things on a movie set. But one of the script clerk's jobs is to make sure the dialogues (the words the actors say) are correct and fit together in each scene. How about helping our script clerk look over the dialogue in John 17? There are some really big words in this scene that we need to make sure the actors understand before we begin our shoot. Let's put those words and what they mean on a cue card to help our actors out.

Glorify is to give honor and praise.
Sanctify is to set apart to make holy.
Unity is the act of being one.
Being one is sticking together with the same purpose and goal.

Now let's take a closer look at our dialogue by looking for the 5 W's and an H. One way an actor prepares himself for his scene is to ask questions. WHAT is my character doing? WHERE is he? WHY did he say that? WHOM is he talking to? WHEN does this take place? HOW does he act? Those are the 5 W's and an H: the WHO, WHAT, WHEN, WHERE, WHY, and HOW questions. Let's take a closer look at what we can find out by asking these questions.

- Asking WHO helps you find out who the people—the characters—are. Who said this or did that?

- WHAT helps you understand what the main things are that happen. What are the characters like, and what do they do?

- WHERE helps you learn where something happened. Where did they go, and where was this said? When we discover a "where" we double-underline the "<u>where</u>" in green.

- WHEN tells us about time, and we mark it with a green clock like this: When did this event happen or when will it happen? When did the main characters do something? It helps us follow the order of events. This is very important in making a movie. We need to make sure we have the correct time an action is taking place. Did this happen at night or in the morning? Knowing when makes sure that we get the shot at the right time.

- WHY asks questions like, Why did he say that? Why did this happen? Why did they go there?

- HOW lets you figure out things like how something is done or how people knew something had happened.

Now let's read John 17 on pages 127-129 and use the 5 W's and an H to prepare for our first shot.

John 17:1 WHO is speaking?

_____

John 17:1 WHOM is He speaking to?

_____

John 17:1 WHAT has happened?
The h ___ ___ ___ has c ___ ___ ___. (Did you mark
it with a clock?)

John 17:1 WHAT does Jesus ask God to do?

_____

Looking at our definition for *glorify* on our cue card on
page 14. WHAT is Jesus asking the Father to do when He
asks Him to "glorify" Him? To give Him h ___ ___ ___ r

John 17:2 WHO has been given authority over all flesh?

_____

John 17:3 WHAT is eternal life? _____

_____

 John 17:4 WHAT did Jesus accomplish?

_____

John 17:5 WHAT glory is Jesus asking the Father to give
Him?

The glory which I had_____

_____

Isn't that awesome? As John 17 begins, we have the awesome privilege of hearing Jesus as He prays to the Father.

WHOM is Jesus praying for in these five verses?
___ ___ ___ ___ ___ ___ ___ (mshlief) (Unscramble the word and place it in the blanks.)

Jesus knows that His hour has come, that He has done everything that the Father has given Him to do, and that He has brought glory to the Father. Now it's time for Him to be given His former glory that He had before He left heaven. Jesus laid aside His glory in heaven to come to this earth to be born, to serve others, to suffer, and to die. He came to do the Father's will.

HONORiNG AND GLORiFYiNG GOD

How about you? Jesus glorified God with His complete obedience.

- Do you honor God by obeying what God says to do in His Word? ____ Yes ____ No

- Are you doing the work God has given you to do? One of the commands God gives children is in Ephesians 6:1-2. Look up these verses in your Bible. WHAT are the commands that God gives children in these verses?

  ___ ___ ___ ___ your parents.

  ___ ___ ___ ___ ___ your father and mother.

WHAT does it mean to obey and honor your parents? If you have done *How to Study Your Bible for Kids*, then you know that to help you fully understand what the author meant when he used the words *obey* and *honor* in Ephesians, you could do a word study. A word study is when you look at the word in the original language in which it was written. Since we are looking at Ephesians, which is in the New Testament, and the New Testament was written in Koine Greek, we would look and see what the Greek words for *obey* and *honor* are in Ephesians 6.

The Greek word for *obey* is *hupakouô* (pronounced hoop-ak-oó-o), which means "to listen, to attend to, to answer, to heed."

So now that you know what *obey* means, do you obey your parents? ____ Yes ____ No

How about honoring them? The Greek word for *honor* is *timaô* (pronounced tim-ah'-o), which means "to fix the value, to price." Do you value your parents and treat them as if they are worth a high price? ____ Yes ____ No

• How do you talk to other people? Do you yell or talk back to your parents? ____ Yes ____ No

• Does your mouth give honor to God? ____ Yes ____ No

• What do you watch on TV? Does what your eyes look at please God and glorify Him? ____ Yes ____ No

• What do you watch that you don't think God would be pleased with? Write it down. Then write out why you don't think it pleases (glorifies or honors) God.

What I Watch	Why God Wouldn't Like It
_____	_____
_____	_____
_____	_____
_____	_____
_____	_____
_____	_____

- Do you care about other people? ____ Yes ____ No

- Name one act of service (doing something for someone out of love—not a job that you are paid for) that you have done for someone.

  _____

- God is your Provider. He gives you what He wants you to have. Do you honor God by being content with the things that you have, or do you always want more?

  _____ I'm content. _____ Sometimes I'm content.

  _____ I want more.

So how did you do? Are you honoring and glorifying God? God wants you to obey Him just like Jesus did. He wants you to share His Word and His love with other people. As we wrap for the day, pray and ask God the Father to help you do the things He has for you to do, to bring glory to His name.

DAY 4

ROLL THOSE CAMERAS!

Our actors are on the set and ready to go. Today we shoot our first scene, and our director needs you to run camera 3. Are you ready? (Have you p ___ ___ ___ ed?) Good—then get behind the camera. We'll need several different shots of this scene. Let's start with a close-up of Jesus as we open and see Him praying to His Father. Then we'll move to a medium shot to show our other characters, the 11 apostles, from the waist up. And as Jesus continues His prayer, we'll do a wide shot showing the whole picture.

"Okay, camera 3, standing by." "Quiet down!" "Roll

sound, roll cameras. Mark it and action." Turn to page 127, and read John 17:6-26.

John 17:6 Look at the key phrase that you marked on your Observation Worksheet. *whom you gave.* WHO are the "these"? WHOM is Jesus praying for?

The _ _ _ _ _ _ _ _ _
(csdilepis)
(We need a medium shot to include these.)

John 17:9 Whose behalf is Jesus asking on?

_____

John 17:11 WHAT is Jesus' prayer request for His disciples? WHAT two things does He specifically ask for?

a. Father, _____ them in _____ _____

b. that they may _____ _____ even as We are.

WHAT does it mean to be one? (Look back at your cue card on page 14.)

_____

John 17:12 WHAT two things did Jesus do for the disciples while He was with them?

a. _____ them in Your name

b. _____ them so not one of them perished

John 17:13 WHAT emotion of Jesus' does He want to be made full in the disciples? His j ____ ____

John 17:14 HOW does the world feel about them? WHY?

_____

_____

WHAT word in John 17 is a contrast to *hate*? A contrast shows us how things are different or opposite. *Good* and *bad*, *black* and *white*, and *night* and *day* are all contrasts. Seeing how things are different (contrasts) is another way to help us study the Bible inductively. Now find the word that is contrasted to *hate* in John 17 (hint: It's a key word). *Hate* is the opposite of _____.

John 17:15 WHAT does Jesus want them kept from? (check one)
❏ the world   ❏ the evil one

John 17:17 WHAT is Jesus' request?

_____

WHAT does that mean? Look back at your cue card on page 14.

_____

So if we are set apart, do we look, think, or act like the world?
____ Yes   ____ No

We are in the world, but we are not to act like the world. WHO should we act like? WHO is our example?

_____

So HOW are we to dress—in the clothes that are the most popular, even if they don't honor God because they are not modest? HOW do we talk? Do we use the language that everyone else uses? After all it's just slang, right? Does it really matter? HOW do we act? Do we make fun of other kids who are different from us?
We need to make sure that we are set apart from the world. We need to check ourselves out to see if we are dressing, talking, and acting in a way that pleases God, or in a way

that is just like the world. Have we compromised so that other people can't tell that we are different from the world?

WHERE do we go for the truth, to show us how to live (speak, dress, and act)?

_____

John 17:18 WHERE has Jesus sent them?

_____

Does Jesus want them to share the gospel with the world?

_____ Yes   _____ No

CHANGE CAMERA ANGLE

Now, as we look at verse 20, we need to change our camera angle. As we discover other people for whom Jesus is praying, we want to make sure that we are shooting a wide shot so that we can get the whole picture.

John 17:20 Jesus is mentioning someone else in His prayer besides the disciples. WHO? WHO are the "those" in this verse?

_____

Amazing! Jesus is praying for all believers (Christians). That's you (if you have accepted Jesus Christ as your Savior), and the whole church—everyone who is a Christian. Did you know that Jesus had prayed for us (Christians) even before we were born? Isn't that awesome? Now let's see what He asks for us in His prayer.

John 17:21-23 WHAT is Jesus' request?

John 17:22 That they _____ _____ _____.

John 17:23 That they may be _____ in _____.

John 17:24 WHAT is Jesus' other request? What is His desire?

_____

Jesus is praying for us to be in heaven with Him so that we can see His glory. Wow! What a gift that God had this prayer included in His Word so that we can see just how much Jesus loves us and cares for us.

Now that you know that Jesus expects you to be one with other believers, should you be getting along with other Christians?
____ Yes   ____ No

Cut! You got some great shots today with camera 3. But before you leave the set, practice your lines for the camera and think about the work Jesus has for you to do (such as being kind to someone at school or sharing the gospel), then do it! Remember, we are to bring glory to His name.

DAY 5

BEHIND THE SCENES

We have gotten a great start on our movie this week! You have been a big help on the set doing background work, checking the script, and running the camera for us.

Today we are going to go behind the scenes and talk about prayer. After all, we have seen the importance of prayer in John 17. Jesus spends an entire chapter praying for Himself, His disciples, and all believers. One of the last things we see Jesus doing on this earth is praying. And we've also talked about how important it is to pray before we study God's Word so that He can lead and guide us.

So WHAT is prayer? Prayer is talking to God. It is building a relationship with Him the way you would with a friend. If you never talk to your friend, will you stay close friends? No. In order to know someone, you have to talk to that person. That's why you need to talk to God, so you can know Him and have a relationship with Him. You also get to know Him by studying His Word, just like you are doing right now. So now that we know the importance of prayer and what prayer is, we need to know how to pray.

Let's go behind the scenes by looking up Luke 11:1 in your Bible. But don't forget to do what first? You guessed it: Pray.

Now read Luke 11:1. WHAT was Jesus doing?

_____

WHAT did one of His disciples ask Him to do?

_____

Luke 11:2-4 is known as "the Lord's Prayer." When Jesus says in verse 2, "When you pray, say..." He is not telling them to just repeat this prayer. He is giving them an example—a pattern to teach them how to pray.

Let's do a cross-reference. That's when you compare Scripture with Scripture. Let's look up Matthew 6:9-13 in your Bible and see what Jesus says about prayer in this passage.

In verse 9 we also see Jesus saying, "Pray, then, in this way." So let's look at this pattern and discover for ourselves how Jesus taught His disciples to pray. Each sentence introduces a topic to pray about. This was the way they remembered what they were to talk to God about.

The first sentence, verse 9, "Our Father who is in heaven, hallowed be Your name," is showing us that when we pray we should start off by praising God for who He is. His name is hallowed—that means it is to be treated as holy, very special. That's why swearing and misusing Jesus' name or God's name is bad! We are to worship God, giving Him the honor He deserves. Tell God you are thankful that He is sovereign. *Sovereign* means God is in control of absolutely everything. Praise Him that He is your Provider and has given you a home, food, clothes, and friends. Just think about the things you know about God, then thank and praise Him for who He is. When you do that, it is called worship.

Verse 10, "Your kingdom come," shows an allegiance to God. Remember how you say the Pledge of Allegiance to the flag of the United States in school? The reason you do this is to show that your allegiance, your loyalty, is to the United States of America. Tell God, "You are my Ruler, and my loyalty is to You and Your kingdom. I will put You first in my life, God. I will talk to You (pray), and read Your Word."

The second part of verse 10, "Your will be done, on earth as it is in heaven," deals with our submission to God and His will. To submit is to obey. Tell God that you are willing to do what He says and do it His way—that you want to please Him. Ask God what He wants, what His plans are, and yield your plans to His.

Verse 11, "Give us this day our daily bread," is where we ask God for our needs. He is our Provider and wants us to come to Him with our needs and desires. God wants us to depend on Him. Tell God what your needs are, such as, "God, I need help on my test. Help me remember what I have studied." Then ask for the needs of other people like your mom and dad, your pastor, your teacher, and friends.

Verse 12, "And forgive us our debts, as we also have forgiven our debtors," is where we confess our sins by telling God what we have done wrong and asking forgiveness for those sins. We also have to forgive those who have treated us wrong. If we are mad at someone because that person has been mean to us and hurt us, Jesus shows us in this verse we are to forgive him or her just like He has forgiven us for the wrong and mean things we have done.

Verse 13 says, "And do not lead us into temptation, but deliver us from evil." If you did our study on James—*Boy, Have I Got Problems!*—you discovered for yourself that God cannot and does not tempt anyone. So we know God would never lead us into temptation. We also know from inductive Bible study that Scripture never contradicts Scripture. So what does this verse mean, "do not lead us into temptation"? This verse is like planning ahead and packing your raincoat so you won't get wet if it rains. You're asking God to help you not give in to sin whenever something happens like being tempted to steal. Your sinful self says, "It's okay. Everyone does it. No one will find out." So when you pray and ask God to not lead you into temptation, say something like this: "God, please help me not to do the things I know are wrong. Help me to obey Your Word. Help me not to yell at my parents when I'm angry, because I know that is sin. Help me to do the right thing even when I am tempted to do wrong. In fact, God, help me stay away from wrong friends and wrong places so I won't be tempted."

The last part of this verse ("For Yours is the kingdom and the power and the glory forever. Amen") is to close your prayer by worshiping God, thanking and praising Him for who He is and what He has done for you. Thank God for listening to your prayers, praise Him for being all-powerful, praise Him that there is no one else like Him and that He will rule forever and ever!

Aren't you excited now that you know God has taught you right in His Word how He wants you to pray? You'll see a prayer list right after this that you can use as you pray for yourself and others. Fill it in, adding any other names of people that you would like to pray for in the blank spaces at the bottom of the chart. Write in the date and your requests. Then, when God answers that prayer, go back and tell how He answered it. But be patient! God answers prayers in His own time and according to His will, so don't be disappointed if the answer doesn't come right away.

Now as we close for the week, spend some time getting to know your heavenly Father. Spend some time in prayer. Use "the Lord's Prayer" as your topic sentences.

Don't forget to worship Him, give Him your loyalty and devotion, give Him control of your life, ask Him for any personal needs and desires, ask Him for the needs of other people, confess your sins, ask for forgiveness, ask Him to help you to forgive others, and ask Him to help you stand firm when temptations come. Then as you close, thank and praise Him for who He is and what He will do.

My Prayer List

Name	Date	Request	How God Answered/ Praise
Mom			
Dad			
brother/sister			
friends			
church			
missionary			
teacher			
me			

IT'S A WRAP!

Well, our opening scene is finished! You did some great work this week checking the background so we would know where to open our scene, making sure we had all the actors' lines down, and you made one terrific cameraperson. As we wrap it up, keep in mind this awesome scene of Jesus praying for you even before you were born! Did you get your lines down? Don't forget that this is a message for you, too. Jesus glorified the Father with His complete obedience, and you need to obey Him, too! Remember what Jesus prayed for you: that you would be one, and that you would be with Him in heaven. Being one means to get along with all believers, not just with your friends. And don't forget what you learned about prayer. Keep on talking to God each day. Next week the suspense builds and the action speeds up as Jesus prepares to lay down His life for us.

2

JOHN 18:1-24

Let's get ready to go! We have a lot of work to do as we move from one location to another this week. The action in our film is about to speed up as we shoot some of the hardest and most heartbreaking scenes in our movie.

We need props, makeup, and costumes, as well as lights, cameras, and reflector boards. And let's not forget our supporting cast. They will play a huge part this week. How about you? Maybe you would like to play a part in one of these scenes. We could sure use you.

But first grab your gear and give the assistant director a hand as she passes out schedules and checks the weather forecast. Then pop in the Jeep and we're off! We've got to get across the Kidron Valley and head for the Mount of Olives.

SCAN THE SCRIPT!

Before we can get started, we need to take a look at our script and get our storyboards ready to go. The storyboards will help prepare the actors and the crew by outlining each scene that we are going to shoot this week.

So scan the script for the events that are happening by turning to pages 129-131 of your Observation Worksheets and reading John 18:1-24. And since we are dealing with different locations, you need to keep your eyes open for each passage that tells you WHERE something is happening. As you read the passage, double-underline each location (the <u>WHERE</u>) that you find in green. That way you will always know where every character plays his or her role. Oh, and don't forget WHO you need to talk to before you begin (God, our Master Director).

Now read John 18:1-24 and draw a picture that describes what is happening in each box below. Then make up a title for each scene, and underneath the title tell <u>WHERE</u> the scene is taking place.

John 18:1-11   John 18:12-14

_____   _____

_____   _____

WHERE: _____   WHERE: _____

John 18:15-18

John 18:19-24

_____

_____

WHERE: _____

WHERE: _____

NOW SHOWING!

So Jesus, knowing all the things that were coming upon Him, went forth and said to them, "Whom do you seek?" They answered Him, "Jesus the Nazarene." He said to them, "I am He." And Judas also, who was betraying Him, was standing with them.

—John 18:4-5

This is your memory verse for the week. The lines show that nothing surprised Jesus. He knew the Father's perfect plan and the role He was to play in it. Practice these lines by saying them out loud three times in a row, three times today.

ON THE MOVE

The storyboards are up and the scene is laid out. How about giving the "grips" a hand as they rig the cameras for our next shoot? We are about to begin a very grueling journey as we film Jesus' last day.

The director is calling us to our places, but before we begin let's pray with the cast and crew. We need to make sure that these scenes honor God, and that we are able to show the world just what Jesus had to go through to save sinners like us.

Looks like we're ready. The director has called on the walkie-talkie. Jesus and His disciples have just left the upper room. So quiet down! The action has begun.

Turn to your Observation Worksheets on page 129 and read John 18:1.

John 18:1 WHERE did Jesus go with His disciples?

_____

Now look at the map on the next page. Today as we take our journey alongside Jesus, we want to show on the map each place that Jesus went. So grab those colored pencils and draw a line with an arrow to follow Jesus' path from the upper room east of Jerusalem over the ravine of the Kidron to the garden called Gethsemane. Then, under that line, put the Scripture (John 18:1) that tells you where He went.

Great footage! We will begin the shoot in the garden just as soon as the gaffer gets all the lights and reflectors set up.

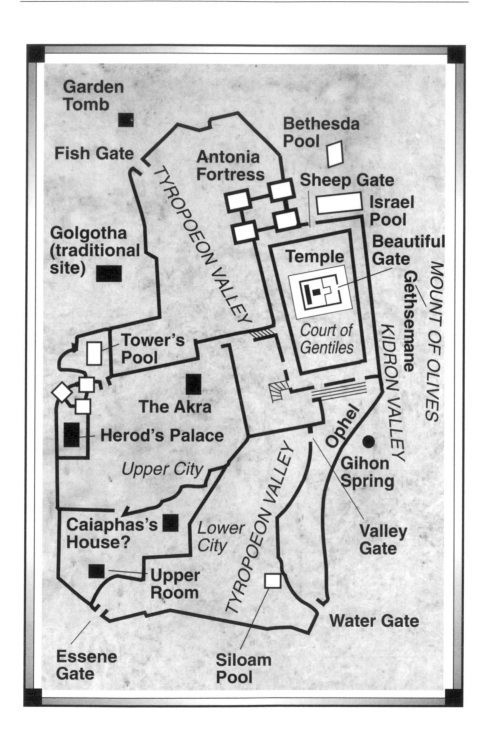

While we're waiting, let's do some cross-referencing, since John doesn't tell us in this passage what Jesus is doing in the garden before He is betrayed. To shoot this scene we need to know what happens in the garden between verse 1 and verse 2 of John 18.

Let's go to Matthew 26:36-47 and read this passage.

Matthew 26:36 WHAT does Jesus tell His disciples once they get to Gethsemane?

_____

Matthew 26:37 WHO are the three that Jesus takes with Him to pray?

_____

(The sons of Zebedee are James and John—Mark 14:33.)

Matthew 26:37-38 WHAT were Jesus' feelings?

_____

Matthew 26:39 WHAT did Jesus pray for?

_____

Matthew 26:40 WHAT were Peter, James, and John doing while Jesus prayed?

_____

Matthew 26:42 Whose will did Jesus want?

_____

Matthew 26:44 HOW many times did Jesus pray?

_____

That was great research. Tomorrow we will do another cross-reference in Luke so we can we make sure we know what was happening in the garden before Judas arrives on the scene. See you then!

MORE RESEARCH

There is another report of Jesus' prayer in the garden in Luke 22:39-47. Let's make sure we understand WHAT Jesus was feeling and going through so we can capture it on film. But before we begin, don't forget to ask God for His help. Then pay special attention to the verses that show us Jesus' feelings. We saw in Matthew that Jesus was deeply grieved even until the point of death. Let's check out what Luke says. We've printed it out below. Read it carefully and <u>double-underline in red</u> everything that shows you what Jesus is going through, how He was feeling.

Luke 22:39-47:
[39] And He came out and proceeded as was His custom to the Mount of Olives; and the disciples also followed Him. [40] When He arrived at the place, He said to them, "Pray that you may not enter into temptation." [41] And He withdrew from them about a stone's throw, and He knelt down and began to pray, [42] saying, "Father, if You are willing, remove this cup from Me; yet not My will, but Yours be done." [43] Now an angel from heaven appeared to Him, strengthening Him. [44] And being in agony He was praying very fervently; and His sweat became like drops of blood, falling down upon the ground. [45] When He rose from prayer, He came to the disciples and found them sleeping from sorrow, [46] and said to them, "Why are you sleeping? Get up and pray that you may not

enter into temptation." [47] While He was still speaking, behold, a crowd came, and the one called Judas, one of the twelve, was preceding them; and he approached Jesus to kiss Him.

Luke 22:43 WHO strengthens Jesus?

_____

Luke 22:44 WHAT emotion was Jesus feeling?

_____

Luke 22:44 WHAT physical thing happens to Jesus' body while He is praying fervently?

_____

Luke 22:45 WHY were the disciples sleeping?

_____

Wow! By looking at the prayer Jesus prayed to the Father, we see the awful agony He went through. Not just the emotional agony, but also the physical agony that was so great that Jesus actually sweat drops of blood, and the Lord sent an angel to Him in order to give Him strength! WHAT did Jesus mean when He asked the Father to let this cup pass from Him?

THE "CUP"

- The cup is Jesus dying on the cross for the sins of the world. Jesus is going to be made sin for us.

- God is going to take every sin that anyone has ever committed and put it on Jesus as He is lifted up on the cross.

- As all the sins of the world are placed on Jesus, God will turn His back on His beloved Son because God is holy and cannot look at sin.

- Drinking the cup means Jesus is going to be separated from His Father not only physically but also spiritually for the first time since the foundation of the world, because "the wages of sin is death"—separation from God and man.

- In the garden Jesus is asking God, wrestling with Him, when He asks for this cup to pass from Him. He's asking, "Father isn't there any other way for Me to do Your will than this?"

- And then He says, "Not my will, but Yours." We see that even in His agony Jesus is willing to drink from the cup and do things God's way. He is willing to obey His Father no matter what the cost. He is glorifying God.

Cut! That was terrific. You captured Jesus' struggle and pain for everyone to see. Now before we wrap it up for the day, why don't you get some of your family or friends and practice this scene. Acting out all that you learned so far will help you to really see what Jesus went through. Oh, and don't forget to rehearse your lines (your memory verse) before you break.

SCENE ONE, TAKE ONE: THE BETRAYAL

Yesterday was quite an emotional scene in the garden. WHAT will take place today? We're about to find out.

"We need more Roman soldiers."

"Where are those costumes?"

"Somebody find those costumes! The soldiers are needed on the set."

The assistant director (the AD) seems to be having a problem. She seems a little frantic, so why don't you lend her a hand making sure our supporting cast is ready to go. Do we have all the costumes and props for the Roman soldiers? It's about time for them to charge onto the scene.

Read John 18:1-12 by turning to your Observation Worksheet on pages 129-130. We need to make sure that we know WHEN these events take place, so put a clock like this: over any words that show you when these events happen.

John 18:2-3 WHO arrives in the garden? And HOW did he know where to find Jesus?

_____

_____

John 18:3 WHO did Judas bring with him?

a. the R _____   c _____

b. the c _____   p _____

c. the P_____

John 18:3 WHAT did they come with (what are our props)?

_____

WHAT time of day was it? (Remember what has been taking place and look at what they are carrying.)

_____ morning   _____ noon   _____ night

John 18:4-7 WHOM are they looking for?

_____

John 18:5 WHO betrays Jesus?

_____

John 18:6 WHAT happens when Jesus says, "I am He"?

_____

John 18:8-9 WHO does Jesus want the soldiers to let go?

_____

John 18:10 WHAT does Peter do?

_____

John 18:11 WHAT does Jesus say to Peter?

_____

John 18:11 WHY does Jesus tell Peter to put away his sword?

_____

John 18:12 WHAT do the Roman cohort, the commander, and the officers of the Jews do?

_____

Cut! What a suspenseful scene! Tomorrow we will follow Jesus to our next location to see where the Roman cohort will take Him.

DAY 5

SCENE TWO, TAKE ONE

"Okay—places, everybody. Is Jesus ready to go? Good—then we're ready to move to our next location. Quiet down, and don't forget to pray!" Read John 18:13-24 by turning to your Observation Worksheet on pages 130-131.

John 18:13 WHERE is Jesus taken?

_____

Now let's go back to our map on page 33. Jesus is on the move again. He is being taken to Annas, the father-in-law of the high priest, Caiaphas. So, using a different colored pencil, draw a line with an arrow from the Garden of Gethsemane back to Caiaphas's house, and put the Scripture verse that tells you where under it.

John 18:15 WHAT happens on the way to Annas's? WHO follows Jesus?

_____

John 18:17 When the slave girl asks Peter if he is one of Jesus' disciples, WHAT does Peter say?

_____

WHY is this important? Let's look at a cross-reference in Matthew. Read Matthew 26:33-34. WHAT does Jesus tell Peter he will do this night before a rooster crows?

_____

John 18:19 WHAT does Annas do when Jesus is taken to him?

Annas q_____ Jesus about His

d_____ and His t_____.

John 18:22 WHAT does the officer do to Jesus?

_____

John 18:23 HOW does Jesus respond?

_____

IT'S A WRAP!

Cut! That was a take. What a long night it has been! Look at everything that has happened so far. First, there was the Lord's Supper. Then Jesus teaches and comforts the disciples (this was in our movie *Jesus— Awesome Power, Awesome Love.* But as we have seen, it is still the same day in our new movie). After that, Jesus prays His high priestly prayer for Himself, the disciples, and all believers. Next He leaves the upper room and walks to the garden, and there He goes through tremendous agony as He prays. Now He's arrested, bound, and led away to Annas, and while He's there, He is struck by an officer. And the night's not over yet. WHAT more will Jesus go through to pay for our sins? We'll find out as we continue His journey next week. As we close, ask yourself:

Would I be willing to lay down my life for my enemies?
____ Yes   ____ No

Am I willing to be slapped, knowing I've done nothing wrong?
____ Yes   ____ No

That's what Jesus did. He laid down His life for the world, His enemies, and took their abuse even though He had done nothing wrong. What incredible love!

3

JESUS ON TRIAL

JOHN 18:24-40

It's great to have you back on the set. As we begin our shoot this week, we will film the final scenes in John 18 as Jesus is put on trial. What an awesome God to allow His Son who did not sin to stand trial, be condemned, and die on the cross so that we might be saved! Let's get started by praying and thanking God for His great mercy and compassion. Then grab your script, and we're ready to plan our storyboards.

SCAN THE SCRIPT!

As we prepare to shoot our final scenes in John 18, we need to study our scripts and sketch our storyboards. Now turn to pages 131-133 to our Observation Worksheets and read John 18:24-40. Don't forget to keep your eyes open for the different locations we will be using for our shoot. Watch for each passage that tells you WHERE something is happening. As you read the passage, double-underline each location (the <u>WHERE</u>) that you find in green.

Now draw a picture that describes what is happening in each box below. Then make up a title for each scene, and underneath the title tell WHERE the scene is taking place.

John 18:25-27   John 18:28-40

_____   _____

_____   _____

WHERE: _____   WHERE: _____

NOW SHOWING!

Therefore Pilate said to Him, "So You are a king?" Jesus answered, "You say correctly that I am a king. For this I have been born, and for this I have come into the world, to testify to the truth. Everyone who is of the truth hears My voice."

—John 18:37

These are your lines (your memory verse for the week). As you memorize them, pretend to be both Pilate and Jesus by changing your voice as you say each of their lines. This will be great practice as you prepare for your role in our movie. And don't forget to say them out loud three times in a row, three times today.

Great rehearsal!

SCENE THREE: THE JEWISH TRIAL

We're back on location, and Jesus has just been questioned by Annas. Let's find out what Annas does with Jesus after he finishes questioning Him. Is everyone on the set? Good—then let's get ready for our next shoot.

Turn to pages 131-132 and read John 18:24-27. Don't forget to mark anything that tells you WHEN these events happen with a clock like this: and double-underline the WHERE in green.

John 18:24 WHERE does Annas send Jesus?

_____

John 18:25 WHAT does Peter say when he is questioned about being Jesus' disciple?

_____

John 18:26-27 WHAT happens when the relative of the slave questions Peter?

_____

John 18:27 WHAT happens immediately after Peter's third denial?

_____

John 18 does not show the details of Jesus being questioned by Caiaphas, so let's take a look at Matthew 26:57-75. Read these verses so you can see just how Jesus was treated during this trial.

Matthew 26:57 WHO was with Caiaphas at this trial?

The s_____ and the e_____

Matthew 26:59 WHAT are the chief priests and the whole Council trying to do?

_____

WHY?_____

WHO is this Council that is at the trial? Find out by taking a look at our cue card.

THE SANHEDRIN

- The Council at Jesus' trial was the Sanhedrin.
- The Sanhedrin was a Jewish governing body that ruled under the power of the high priest. The high priest was like the president of this Jewish body.
- The Sanhedrin would rule and make decisions on religious matters, but they were under the authority of the Roman government.
- The Roman government gave the Sanhedrin the right and power to judge and enforce their laws. But the Sanhedrin did not have the authority to condemn people to death.

Matthew 26:63 HOW did Jesus respond?

_____

Matthew 26:64 WHO does Jesus say they will see hereafter?

"The _____ of _____ sitting at the right hand of _____, and _____ on the _____ of _____."

Matthew 26:65 WHAT is the high priest's response?

_____

Matthew 26:67 HOW is Jesus treated?

_____

Isn't it heartbreaking to see how harshly Jesus was treated at His trial? Tomorrow we will take a look at Mark's account of this same trial. Hang in there. You are doing a great job. And don't forget to "run those lines."

THE TRIAL CONTINUES

As we continue our shoot on the Jewish trial, let's do a cross-reference. Let's find out what Mark has to say about this very same trial that we looked at in Matthew. Look up and read Mark 14:53-65. Then make a list below of each event that happens. We've done the first one for you.

Mark 14:53 Jesus is led to the high priest and all the chief priests, elders, and scribes.

Mark 14:54 _____

Mark 14:55 _____

Mark 14:61 _____

Mark 14:62 _____

Mark 14:63-64 _____

Mark 14:65 _____

So do Mark and Matthew agree on what happened at the Jewish trial? _____ Yes   _____ No

Absolutely! Isn't that awesome how Scripture never contradicts Scripture? Instead, when we look at different passages in the Bible (cross-referencing) we are able to get a clearer understanding of what the Bible says.

Now why don't you draw a picture of this incredible trial in the box below? Show Caiaphas, the chief priests, the elders, and the scribes (and don't forget Peter lurking in the background by the fire). Show the different emotions in the faces of the people. Are they happy, sad, scared, or angry? Show how Jesus is treated in Mark 14:65.

Now let's take a look at some facts. Check out the cue card below to see if those who were accusing Jesus of breaking the law broke any laws themselves.

RiGHT OR WRONG?

- Did you know that when Jesus was arrested in the garden it was illegal to bind Him since He did not resist His arrest?

- Did you know that it was illegal to have a Jewish trial at night? It was to be held in the daytime.

- Did you know that the first thing in a Jewish trial was for all the witnesses to be questioned? It was illegal for a person to be a witness against himself (such as when Caiaphas questioned Jesus instead of questioning witnesses).

- Did you know that it was illegal for Jesus to be hit by a guard while He was being questioned (John 18:22)?

- Did you know that it was illegal for a man to be condemned to death the same day as his trial?

Amazing, isn't it, that the very ones who were so angry with Jesus for breaking their laws, broke their own laws to try and get rid of Him.

Now the cock has crowed and early morning has arrived.

So WHERE did Jesus spend the night?

Great work! As you leave the set today, don't forget to rehearse your lines one more time. The more you rehearse, the better your performance will be at the end of the week.

LET'S MARK THE SCENE

Early morning has arrived and Jesus is about to be moved again. But before we head out for our next location, let's take a closer look at our script. Now turn to pages 132-133, and read John 18:28-40. Mark the following key words on your Observation Worksheet. (Remember to keep your eyes open for anything that tells you WHEN and mark it like this: 🕐 and mark WHERE by double-underlining the <u>WHERE</u> in green.)

Truth (draw in purple and color it green)

King and kingdom (draw in purple and color it blue)

Now "run those lines." You should have them down by now!

SCENE FOUR: THE ROMAN TRIAL

What a week! We have shot some heartbreaking moments as we've watched Jesus being beaten and spit on. A.K., our makeup girl, needs your help. She has quite a job ahead to show what Jesus looked like after being slapped, spit on, and beaten. And as the next scenes unfold, it's sure to get much worse. Are you up to the job? Don't forget to pray, and then head back to John 18 on pages 129-133.

Read John 18:28-40 and do the crossword puzzle below.

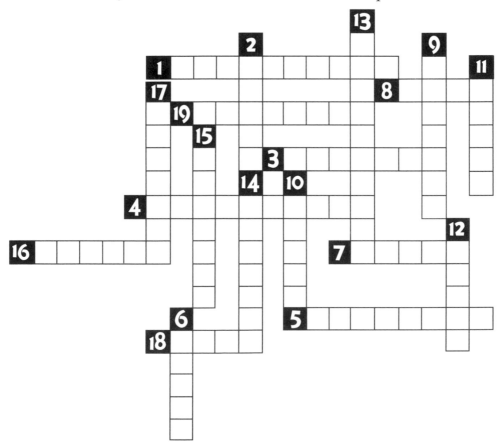

1. **(Across)** John 18:28 WHERE does Caiaphas send Jesus? To the _____

   Go back to your map on page 33. Use a different colored pencil and draw a line with an arrow from Caiaphas's house to the Praetorium where Jesus is taken. The Praetorium was used as a temporary Roman military headquarters or as the palace in Jerusalem to house the Roman governor. It was either a building next to Herod's palace or the Antonia Fortress beside the temple mount complex. Draw your line to the Antonia Fortress. Don't forget to put the Scripture verse under the line that tells you where Jesus was taken.

2. **(Down)** John 18:28 WHAT time of day is it? It was

   _____.

3. **(Across)** John 18:28 WHY didn't the Jews enter the Praetorium? So they would not be_____ but might eat the Passover.

4. **(Across)** John 18:29 WHAT did Pilate ask the Jews? "What _____ do you bring against this Man?"

5. **(Across)** Read Matthew 27:2 WHO is Pilate? The_____

6. **(Down)** John 18:31 WHAT did Pilate tell the Jews to do? "Take Him yourselves, and _____ Him according to your law."

7. **(Across)** John 18:31 WHAT was the Jews' response? "We are not permitted to put anyone to _____."

8. **(Across)** John 18:33 WHAT question did Pilate ask Jesus? "Are You the _____ of the Jews?"

9. **(Down)** John 18:36 WHAT does Jesus tell Pilate is not of this world and realm? His _____

10. **(Down)** John 18:37 WHAT reason does Jesus tell Pilate that He came into the world? To testify to the _____

11. **(Down)** John 18:38 WHAT did Pilate tell the Jews? "I find no _____ in Him."

Now, the Gospel of John doesn't tell us that Jesus was taken somewhere else after Pilate questions Him, but Luke does. So let's go to Luke and read Luke 23:1-7. Then answer the questions.

12. **(Down)** Luke 23:7 WHERE does Pilate send Jesus? To _____

Pilate sends Jesus to Herod because he finds out that Jesus belongs to Herod's jurisdiction. Now draw another line on your map from the Antonia Fortress to Herod's palace.

Read Luke 23:8-12

13. **(Down)** Luke 23:9 WHAT did Herod do? He _____ Him at some length.

14. **(Down)** Luke 23:10 WHO was there accusing Jesus? The chief priests and the _____

15. **(Down)** Luke 23:11 HOW did Herod and his soldiers treat Jesus? With contempt and _____ Him

16. **(Across)** Luke 23:11 WHERE does Herod send Jesus? Back to _____

Now go back to your map and draw your line from Herod's palace back to Pilate at the Antonia Fortress.

Let's go back to John 18 and take a look at the last three verses.

17. **(Down)** John 18:38-39 WHAT is the custom that Pilate is referring to? To _____ someone at Passover

18. **(Across)** John 18:39 WHO does Pilate offer to release? The King of the _____

19. **(Across)** John 18:40 WHO does the crowd want?_____

CHARACTER PROFILE: WHO IS HEROD?

- Herod the Great was a king appointed by the Roman senate. He ruled from 37–4 B.C. He was known as the "King of the Jews," even though the Jews hated him.

- He was a cruel man who felt threatened when the wise men came to worship Jesus, so he ordered the murder of all male children in Bethlehem who were two years old and under.

- After Herod the Great dies, his kingdom is divided, and each of his four sons is given a fourth of his kingdom to rule. They are called *tetrarch*, which means "a fourth."

- Herod Antipas is the son of Herod the Great, the tetrarch over Galilee and Perea. He ruled from 4 B.C.–A.D. 39. He is the Herod we see in Matthew 14:1-11; Luke 3:1,19; 13:31-33; 23:7-12.

- Herod Antipas is in Jerusalem at the time of Jesus' trial because of the Passover celebration.

- Once Pilate discovered that Jesus was a Galilean, he realized that Jesus would fall under Herod Antipas's rule. So he sends Jesus to Herod hoping that Herod will take care of his problem of what to do with Jesus (Luke 23:5-7).

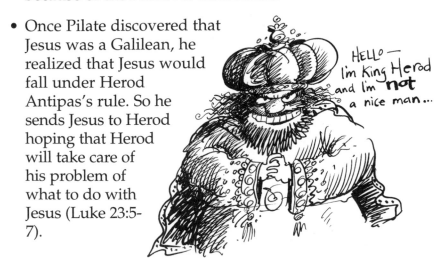

- Herod is curious about Jesus and mistreats Him. He then sends Jesus back to Pilate because he also finds no guilt in Him.

Whew! That was quite a scene. Did you get your lines down this week? Why don't you say them to a grown-up? Show what a great actor or actress you are by acting out your lines and changing your voice like you did at rehearsal.

Then why don't you get your whole family together and play a game of charades? Use the scenes in John 18 of Jesus praying, being betrayed, denied, tried, beaten, and shuffled from one place to another. Make two teams. Let one person act a scene out, and let everyone else guess who that person is and what that person is doing. Take turns between the two teams, alternating who acts and who guesses. Each correct guess is worth 5 points, and the team with the most points wins!

IT'S A WRAP!

How did you like working on location this week? It was grueling, dirty, and heartbreaking work, but what an amazing job you did capturing these very important scenes on film for other people to see.

As we wrap it up this week, things are pretty tense. Pilate wants to release Jesus, but the crowd is against it. What will Pilate do? Will he give in to the pressure of the crowd, or will he do the right thing? Remember, Pilate has just told the crowd, "I find no guilt in Him." So what choice will he make? We'll find out as we continue making our movie. But as you leave the set, put yourself in Pilate's place.

Has anyone ever wanted you to do something, yet in your heart you knew it was wrong? _____ Yes _____ No

How did you feel? _____

What did you do?_____

Did you give in to the "crowd" (your peers, the kids watching you), or did you stand for what you knew was right?

_____

Take some time and think about this before you leave the set. Pray and ask God to help you to do the right thing, and to give you strength to not give in to what other people want you to do!

It's a wrap!

4

THE ROAD TO CALVARY

JOHN 19

The director is busy preparing for our shoot today. How about you—are you ready to go? Make sure you spend some time talking with God.

These scenes will be the hardest of all the scenes we've filmed. It's sure to get very quiet and emotional on the set as we shoot the scenes that show what a high price Jesus paid for our salvation.

SCAN THE SCRIPT!

"Storyboards—where are those storyboards? I need those storyboards so I can plan this shoot."

Help! The director is searching for the storyboards for John 19. Let's turn to page 133 of our Observation Worksheets and get to work creating those storyboards right away!

Read John 19 and draw a picture in each box below that describes what is happening.

Remember to keep your eyes open for each passage that

tells you WHERE something is happening. As you read the passage, double-underline each location (the <u>WHERE</u>) that you find in green.

Then make up a title for each scene, and underneath the title tell where the scene is taking place.

John 19:1-16

_____

_____

WHERE: _____

John 19:17-30

_____

_____

WHERE: _____

John 19:31-37

_____

_____

WHERE: _____

John 19:38-42

_____

_____

WHERE: _____

Great work! You got those finished just in time because here comes the director. And it looks like he has another special project for you to do.

Awesome! He wants you to be Jesus' stand-in. That means you'll get to pretend to be Jesus while they are setting up the shots for the cameraperson, and you will actually get to practice Jesus' final words on the cross.

Why don't you get started on your lines by rehearsing them right now? Write them out on your cue card (an index card). How many times in a row should you say them aloud? _____ times   And how many times today? _____ times

---

NOW SHOWING!

Therefore when Jesus had received the sour wine, He said, "It is finished!" And He bowed His head and gave up His spirit.

—John 19:30

These are powerful words that have to do with you! We'll take a closer look at what Jesus meant as we continue our shoot this week. See you then!

DAY 2

PROPS AND MAKEUP!

We're back at the Praetorium, and it sounds like the assistant director (AD) could use some help with the supporting cast and extras.

"Get those crowds ready. Are they ready for their big scene? We need makeup, costumes, and props."

Grab the glue, paraffin, fake blood, and dirt to help A.K., the makeup girl, get Jesus ready for the scourging that is about to take place.

This will be painful to think about and do. But we need our movie to show the world what Jesus really looked like, what He went through, and what it cost Him to forgive our sins.

The director is calling Pilate and Jesus to the set. Check and see if the AD has the crowd ready, and then turn to John 19 on page 133 and read John 19:1-3.

WHAT did Pilate do with Jesus? He _____ Him.

Let's take a look at our cue card below to see what it means to be scourged.

CRACKING THE WHIP!

- A scourge was a type of whip.

- It was a stick with leather straps on it. Sometimes it had as many as nine leather straps on it and was called a cat-o'-nine-tails.

- The whip would have metal and pieces of bone attached to the straps. As the person was whipped, the jagged edges would catch and tear into the person's flesh.

- The metal was sometimes a ball that would cause sores and bleeding inside the body.

- The Jewish law said that a person could not be whipped more than 40 times.

- But the Romans did not have this law and could beat the person to any degree as long as they kept him alive. Because of this, we do not know how many times the Roman soldiers whipped Jesus, but it was probably a lot more than 40 times!

- A person about to be crucified was scourged (beaten) in order to weaken him so that it would not take him so long to die on the cross.

John 19:2 WHAT two props do we need for Jesus?

a. _____

b. _____

John 19:3 HOW is Jesus treated by the soldiers?
They came up to Him and said, "_____,
_____ of the _____" and gave Him

_____ _____ _____ _____.

Now after Jesus is scourged, mocked, and slapped, Pilate brings Him out again in John 19:4. As we get ready to film our next scene, let's see WHAT Pilate tells the crowd. Find out by looking at the puzzle below.

Sometimes a movie will have some very famous lines that the moviegoer doesn't forget. To uncover Pilate's famous line, solve the puzzle by coloring the spaces red that have a dot in them. Let's find out WHAT Pilate tells the crowd about Jesus.

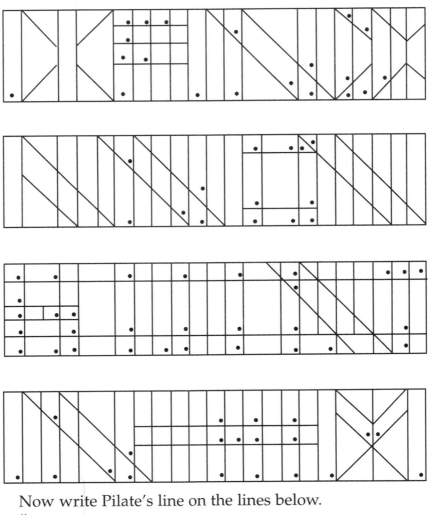

Now write Pilate's line on the lines below.

"_____ _____ _____ _____

_____ _____."

Amazing, isn't it, how someone who isn't guilty can be treated worse than the very worst criminals? Did Jesus have to take the punishment since He committed no sin? _____ Yes _____ No

Of course not! Look at 1 Peter 2:24 to see WHY Jesus chose to die. It was His choice—no one made Him do it! Tell WHY on the lines below.

_____

_____

Let's look at another passage, Isaiah 53:6, that shows WHAT we did to cause Jesus to make this choice. Read Isaiah 53:6. WHAT is Jesus comparing us to in this verse?

A *comparison* is when you look at how things are alike—like saying, "David runs like a jackrabbit." By comparing David's speed when he runs to a jackrabbit's, it gives us an idea of how fast David can run.

So WHAT does Jesus compare us to?

_____

If you did *Jesus in the Spotlight,* then you know from learning about sheep that they are very stubborn and need a shepherd to guide them. So WHAT happens to the sheep in this verse?

They have _____ _____.

WHAT have we done? Each of us has
_____ to _____ _____
_____.

WHOM did God cause our iniquity to fall on?

_____

It's important to understand that Jesus made the choice to die on the cross not because He did anything wrong, but because we did. There was no guilt found in Him! He died for the whole world's sins.

QUIET ON THE SET!

Now that we're back on the set, let's go to pages 133-134 and read John 19:6-16 to find out what happens after Pilate scourges Jesus and brings Him back out to the crowd.

"Is the crowd ready to shoot their scene? All right, quiet down! Roll those cameras. Action!"

John 19:6 Cue the chief priests and the officers with their line. WHAT do they say when they see Jesus?

_____

John 19:6 And WHAT is Pilate's response?

"Take Him _____ and

_____ Him, for I _____

_____ _____ _____ _____."

John 19:7 WHAT did Jesus say He was that made the Jews think He should die?

That He was the _____ of _____

John 19:8 HOW does this make Pilate feel?
a. happy   b. angry   c. afraid   d. sad

John 19:9-11 WHO did Jesus say had given Pilate authority over Him?

_____

John 19:12-13 Did Pilate make an effort to release Jesus?
____ Yes   ____ No

John 19:14 WHAT day and hour is it?

_____

Now go to your Observation Worksheet on page 134 and mark what day and hour it is with a clock like this: ⏰ In Roman time this would have been around 6:00 in the morning when Pilate brought Jesus out.

Hold back the crowd. They are getting pretty upset. Can you hear their anger?

John 19:15 WHAT are they chanting?

_____

John 19:16 So WHAT does Pilate do?

_____

Cut! Wrap it up. That's it for the day.
    Don't forget, the cameraperson will be using you to set up for Jesus' shot pretty soon. Have you learned your lines yet? Practice them one more time!

Now as we close, was Pilate strong and able to stand firm, or was he a weak coward? Write your answer below and tell why you think that.

_____

_____

THE DEATH SCENE

Things are pretty quiet on the set this morning. Everyone is feeling the weight of filming the death scene. Let's pray for wisdom and direction as we prepare for our opening shot.

We saw yesterday that it was the day of preparation for the Passover. Do you remember what you learned in *Jesus— Awesome Power, Awesome Love* about the feast of Passover? The feast of Passover was a very special holy day for the Jews. It was a reminder of God's rescue of the children of Israel from slavery in Egypt when the angel of God saw the blood on the doorposts of their houses and passed over them, letting their children live.

To celebrate this feast they sacrificed an unblemished male lamb. Now here we are at Passover, and WHO are the Jews about to crucify? Jesus. God gave the Jews the feast of Passover to show them a picture of Jesus—the perfect, unblemished Lamb of God to be sacrificed to take our sins so that we can have life.

Now the director is ready. The time has come as a hush falls on the set and our cast gathers to play out the most important moment in all of history. Turn to pages 134-136 of your Observation Worksheet and read John 19:16-37.

John 19:17 WHERE was Jesus taken? Write it out and then double-underline the place in green on your Observation Worksheet.

_____

John 19:18 WHAT happens to Jesus?

They _____ Him.

A CRIMINAL'S DEATH

Death by crucifixion was used for the lowest of criminals.

It was the most cruel, shameful, and painful way to put a criminal to death. The Roman law said that no Roman citizen could be crucified.

First the victim was scourged (beaten) to weaken him so that it would shorten the time it would take for him to die on the cross.

Then the victim had to carry his crossbeam to the place he would be crucified. (We see Jesus carrying His crossbeam in John 19:17 before the soldiers enlisted Simon to carry it the rest of the way—read this in Matthew 27:32.)

The victim would either be tied or nailed to the cross. Jesus' wrists and feet were nailed with spikes to the wooden cross. As the victim hung on the cross, all of his weight would pull on his wrists and feet as he tried to hold up his whole body.

There was also a foot piece on the cross that allowed the victim to push himself up so he could take a breath and stay alive. It was agonizing and painful to push up the body to take that breath. The victim would die when he could no longer lift himself up to take that breath of air.

It was a slow, horrible death of shame, rejection, and suffering.

John 19:19 WHAT was the inscription Pilate wrote and put on the cross? "Jesus the _____, the

_____ _____ _____ _____"

John 19:20-22 Were the chief priests of the Jews happy with what Pilate wrote on Jesus' sign?

____ Yes ____ No

John 19:23-24 WHAT did the soldiers do when they crucified Jesus?

Took His outer _____ and made _____

_____, and for His tunic they c_____

l_____ to decide whose it would be.

John 19:25 WHO witnessed Jesus' death on the cross?

_____

John 19:26-27 WHO does Jesus take care of while He is dying on the cross?

_____

John 19:28-29 WHAT did they give Jesus to drink?

_____

John 19:30 WHAT did Jesus say?

_____

John 19:30 After Jesus says this, WHAT does He do?

_____

TETELESTAI

Tetelestai is the Greek word for "It is finished," Jesus' final words before He gives up His spirit and dies.

In Bible times when a man had a debt that he could not pay right away, he wrote on a piece of paper what he owed. The person that he owed the debt to would keep that piece of paper until the man could pay his debt.

Once the man paid off his debt, the person holding the piece of paper would write *tetelestai* across the paper, which meant "paid in full." Then he would nail the paper to the door of the man's house so everyone could see his debt was paid.

When Jesus said, "It is finished," He was saying that He had paid our debt in full. The Old Testament sacrifices could not take away sin. They could only cover it up (Hebrews 10:3-4).

Did you know that at the very time that Jesus was crucified on the cross, the Jews were sacrificing their Passover lambs for the feast of Passover? Right in front of them, Jesus—the perfect, willing Lamb of God—shed His blood and laid down His life, taking away all the sins of the world (John 1:29; Hebrews 10:10-12). Jesus paid our debt in full. What awesome, amazing love!

Wow! Those are some powerful scenes, but there are some pretty amazing supernatural events that also took place during Jesus' death that John doesn't tell us about. Our special-effects guy wants you to help him re-create these events for our movie, so let's head over to Matthew and find out what happens during Jesus' crucifixion. What special effects do we need? Read Matthew 27:45-54.

Now let's list the supernatural events that happened at the cross.

Matthew 27:45 _____ fell upon all the land.

Matthew 27:51 The _____ of the _____

was _____ in _____ from _____ to

_____, the _____

_____, and the rocks were _____.

Matthew 27:52 The _____ were opened, and

many _____ of the saints who had fallen

asleep were _____.

Matthew 27:54 HOW did the centurion feel when he
saw these events?

_____ happy   _____ sad   _____ afraid

WHAT did the centurion say?

_____

Our audience is sure to be amazed. What an awesome,
powerful God! He controls all things in heaven and earth!

Now as we get ready to close the set for the day, we need
to realize that as horrible as these events were, they did not
surprise God or Jesus. Check out the Old Testament prophe-
cies that told us hundreds of years ago, before the crucifixion
ever happened, how Jesus would suffer for us. Look up Isaiah
50:6; Psalm 22:14-18; and Isaiah 52:14 and read each of these
passages. Then match the descriptions below of what happened to Jesus with the verses that you found them in. You
will use some of the verses more than once.

1. _____ poured out like water   a. Isaiah 50:6

2. _____ strength dried up   b. Psalm 22:18

3. _____ appearance marred more than   c. Psalm 22:14

    any other man   d. Isaiah 52:14

4. _____ beard plucked out   e. Psalm 22:17

5. _____ count my bones   f. Psalm 22:15

6. _____ tongue cleaves to jaws

7. _____ humiliated and spit upon

8. _____ heart like wax, melted within me

9. _____ divided my garments, cast lots

for my clothing

10. _____ gave His back to those who struck Him

11. _____ bones are out of joint

Isn't it amazing how everything that was prophesied long ago in the Old Testament was fulfilled in the New Testament?

Isaiah 52:14 tells us that Jesus' appearance was marred more than any other man's when He went to the cross. He didn't even look like a man! He was so battered and beaten. Can you even imagine the pain He suffered for you and me?

There is a great video series called *The Visual Bible*, which has four videos in the set on the book of Matthew. Every word in Matthew is taken straight from the New International Version Bible. In the last video you can see for yourself how Jesus was treated and the high price He paid for our sins.

The actor who plays Jesus, Bruce Marchiano, has written a book called *In the Footsteps of Jesus*. In this book Bruce describes what it felt like when he was made up to look horribly bruised and battered for the crucifixion scenes. He says it was awful. He felt such shame and ugliness, and people were disgusted just looking at him. He said he had never felt so naked and alone, and he was only play-acting. If Bruce was so devastated just pretending to be Jesus, can you imagine what it must have felt like to be Jesus?

As we leave the set today, why don't you go to Jesus in prayer and thank Him for the price He paid for your sins? Thank Him for giving up His place in heaven, coming to live on this earth, ministering, teaching, loving, suffering, and dying so we can be with Him forever and ever for all ETERNITY! Praise God for His precious Son!

BEHIND THE SCENES

As we finish up the scenes of Jesus' crucifixion and His burial, we need you to give our prop guy a hand. We'll need some different props on the set today.

Our last scene was of Jesus' final words and the supernatural events that took place. By the way, you did a great job standing in for Jesus to help set that scene. Why don't you say those lines one more time to a grown-up today?

Now let's open our scene on page 136 by reading John 19:31-42.

Answer the 5 W's and an H below, and then find the answers in the word search.

John 19:31 WHY did Pilate ask that their legs be broken? So that the bodies would not remain on the cross on the

_____

John 19:33 Did they break Jesus' legs? ____ Yes ____ No

WHY or why not? Because they saw that Jesus was already _____

John 19:34 WHAT did they do to Jesus? (You need one of your props for this scene.) "One of the soldiers

_____ His side with a _____,

and immediately _____ and _____ came out."

John 19:36 Was the prophecy in Scripture about Jesus' death fulfilled? ____ Yes ____ No

John 19:37 WHAT was the other prophecy about Jesus that was fulfilled? "They shall _____ on Him whom they pierced."

John 19:38 WHO asked Pilate for Jesus' body?
_____ of Arimathea

John 19:38 WHO was Joseph?
A s_____ d_____ of Jesus

John 19:39 WHO else helped Joseph? (Remember, he came to Jesus in John 3.)

_____

John 19:39 WHAT did he bring with him? (more props)
A mixture of _____ and _____

John 19:39 HOW much did they weigh?
About a _____ _____

John 19:40 WHAT did they do with Jesus' body?
Bound it in _____ _____
with the _____

John 19:41 WHERE did they lay Jesus? (Don't forget to double-underline this place in green on your work-sheet.)
In the _____ in a new _____

John 19:42 WHY did they choose a nearby tomb?

Because it was the _____ _____ of

_____

Now find all the answers you just wrote in the blanks in the word search below.

N	O	I	T	A	R	A	P	E	R	P	W
I	S	P	E	A	R	A	I	L	D	O	A
C	S	G	L	J	O	S	E	P	H	U	T
O	D	A	N	O	P	K	R	I	R	N	E
D	A	R	B	I	O	W	C	C	R	D	R
E	Y	D	C	B	P	K	E	S	Y	S	S
M	D	E	A	D	A	P	D	I	M	E	D
U	S	N	K	W	P	T	A	D	C	O	L
S	D	E	R	D	N	U	H	R	O	T	I
J	E	W	I	S	H	V	E	L	W	O	N
A	L	O	E	S	U	T	B	R	Z	M	E
L	I	A	Z	R	E	W	S	E	M	B	N

Wow! Since you did such a great job working with our prop guy, we thought it might be fun for you to make some props of your own. Use your props to share the story of Jesus' arrest, trial, death, and resurrection.

First you will need some colored plastic Easter eggs. You can make as many as you want, but you'll need at least six.

Then you need to make or buy some props that you can fit inside the eggs to help tell Jesus' story.

Some ideas for props are:

- Draw a cup or praying hands (for the cup Jesus prayed about).

- A Hershey kiss (for Judas's kiss of betrayal).

- A coin (the 30 pieces of silver Judas betrayed Jesus for).

- A piece of rope (to bind Jesus with).

- Draw a rooster (Peter's denial).

- Draw or cut a piece of leather (for the whip used to scourge Jesus).

- Draw or use a piece of purple cloth (Jesus' robe).

- Make a crown out of grapevine or a vine (the crown of thorns).

- Draw or make a cross.

- A small nail (for the nails that pierced Jesus' hands and feet).

- Use a piece of gauze or white linen (to wrap Jesus' body).

- Mom may have some spices in her cabinet like cloves (for the spices to wrap Jesus' body).

- A rock (for the stone that was rolled away).

- Leave one egg empty (the tomb was empty).

- A balloon or a piece of cotton (for Jesus' ascension into heaven).

- Draw or make a red heart (you could use a pipe cleaner—to show God and Jesus' love for a sinner like you and me).

Use your imagination and have fun!

Once you have all your props made, put them inside your eggs and number each egg with a magic marker.

Hide the eggs and get your family and friends to help you find them.

After you find all the eggs, tell Jesus' story, having each person open the eggs that he or she found, one at a time, starting with egg number 1, and talk about what that prop means. This a fun way to share with other people what Jesus did for us.

IT'S A WRAP!

You did it! It was a very hard and painful week to watch Jesus suffer and die, but you were able to capture the heartbreak and suffering for our movie audience. Now we can show the whole world that we are all sinners (like sheep who have gone astray), and that the only way to be saved from those sins is through Jesus Christ's (our Passover Lamb) sacrifice of dying on the cross.

As we wrap it up, why don't you take a moment and think about that sacrifice? Have you accepted God's gift of salvation? When you do, you need to realize that you are a sinner and have hurt God greatly. Then you need to tell God you want to be set free from your sin, that you want to be a follower of Jesus Christ for the rest of your life. If this is your desire, then tell God you believe Jesus is God's Son and you want to receive Him as Savior. When you do, God will make you His child, and Jesus and the Holy Spirit will come to live in you. Remember John 14:23. You will live forever because Jesus died and rose from the dead. When you receive Jesus you will want to "confess" Him before other people. That means to tell others you have truly believed in Jesus Christ and now belong to Him. You will also want to share with someone else what Jesus did and give that person the chance to receive God's gift of salvation, to have eternal life (John 3:16).

Now as you leave the set for the week, sing a praise song to Jesus to thank Him for what He did for you and me.

It's a wrap!

5

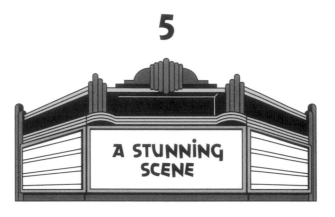

JOHN 20

Hurry! Quick! Run to the tomb! Our sorrow is about to be turned into joy this week. We are going to film the most dramatic and stunning scene in all of history! There's not a moment to lose! But before you run off, make sure you spend some time talking to your Master Director so that He will direct and bless all your hard work.

SCAN THE SCRIPT!

We have been brokenhearted the last two weeks watching Jesus suffer. As we left our location at Calvary, Jesus has died. Joseph of Arimathea and Nicodemus have taken His body to the tomb and wrapped it with 100 pounds of spices in linen wrappings.

WHAT will happen next? Let's find out! Grab those colored pencils and your script of John 20 on pages 137-140. Read John 20, and then capture these events on your storyboards. And don't forget to write a title underneath each storyboard to describe the event.

John 20:1-10

_____

_____

WHERE: _____

John 20:11-18

_____

_____

WHERE: _____

John 20:19-23

_____

_____

WHERE: _____

John 20:24-31

_____

_____

WHERE: _____

Awesome storyboards! Now our director has some very important lines that he wants you to share with the world. You've heard these before; in fact, we talked about them on the very first day on the set of our movie. These lines are the reason that John wrote the Gospel of John, and they are found in our script (John 20) this week.

Instead of just handing you the script to review your lines, our art director wanted to show off just a little bit. As you can guess, he is a pretty artistic guy who loves to create. Guess what? He has created a rebus of these very famous lines that you'll be memorizing (if you learned them in our last movie, you will be reviewing them this week).

A rebus is a word puzzle that mixes pictures and words. When you combine the pictures and the letters by adding or subtracting letters, you will end up with a new word.

So make our art director feel great by figuring out his creative masterpiece and writing out the solution on the lines underneath the puzzle. After you have solved the rebus, don't forget to look in your script to find the address of this verse.

BUT THESE HAVE 🐝+N

✏-E+IO SO T+🎩 YOU

[MAY] 🐝-E+🛝-S-D 🍂-LEAS

T+🎩 JESUS IS [spool]-RAD

[DEC 25 🎄]-MAS THE ☀-U+O

[ON/OFF]-F GOD; [hand]-H T+🎩

🐝-E+LIEVING YOU

[MAY] HAVE -LIFE- IN

HIS N+[camel]-C-L.

_____

_____

_____

John 20: _____

Then rehearse those lines three times today.

Famous Lines

Before we shoot the spectacular events we just drew for our storyboards, let's go back and look at the things that Jesus had told His disciples while He was alive and ministering to them. What were His words to them? Let's find out by pulling out the master script (our Bible) and looking up the following passages.

Read Matthew 16:20-21. WHAT did Jesus start showing His disciples?

That He must go WHERE? To _____

and _____ many things from the _____

and _____ _____ and _____,

and be _____, and be _____ _____

WHEN? On the _____ day

Read Mark 8:31. Jesus is teaching the disciples.

HOW do Jesus' teachings in this verse compare to the things He shows them in Matthew 16? Do both of these verses say the same thing? _____ Yes _____ No

Read John 2:18-22.

John 2:18 WHAT are the Jews asking Jesus for, to show His authority? A s_____

John 2:19 HOW did Jesus answer them?

_____

_____

HOW many days did Jesus say? _____ days

John 2:20 Did the Jews believe Jesus?____ Yes   ____ No

John 2:21 WHAT was Jesus talking about when He used the word *temple?* Did He mean the actual temple, or was He talking about something else? Tell WHAT Jesus meant when He said He would raise the temple in three days.

_____

These are some very important lines because they show that Jesus knew what was going to happen. He was not surprised or confused by the things that happened to Him. Jesus told His disciples what would take place. He knew He would suffer and die, but He also knew WHAT would happen three days later, right? He would be _____.

Now take a look at one more passage. Let's see if Jesus told anyone else that He was going to rise from the dead in three days. Read Matthew 27:62-66.

Matthew 27:62 WHO got together to discuss Jesus' death the day after the preparation?

_____

Matthew 27:63 WHAT had they remembered?

_____

Matthew 27:64 WHAT did they want?

The _____ to be made _____

For HOW long? Until after the _____ _____

WHY? They didn't want the disciples to come and

_____ _____ _____ and

tell the people Jesus had _____ from the

_____.

Matthew 27:65 Did Pilate give them permission for a
guard? ____ Yes   ____ No

Matthew 26:66 HOW did they make the grave secure?

_____

So we see that these enemies of Jesus had listened to the
things that Jesus said and were determined to do everything
in their power to keep Jesus from coming back. But WHO is
more powerful? You know WHO. WHO is the only one that
can overcome death?
    Spell it out with a shout!   ____ ____ ____ ____ ____

Now practice those famous lines of yours. The director
wants you to stand up and deliver those lines at the end of
our scene this week.

SpECiAL EffEcTs

Here we go. We're almost ready to roll. Thanks for helping
our special-effects guy once again. Shhh! The assistant director
is calling everyone to the set. Before we shoot the scenes in
John 20, we need to film a few scenes in Matthew. Matthew
shows us the special effects that happen right before the scene
in John 20 begins.

So let's turn to Matthew 28 and read verses 1 through 15 to set the scene.

Now roll those cameras by doing the crossword puzzle below.

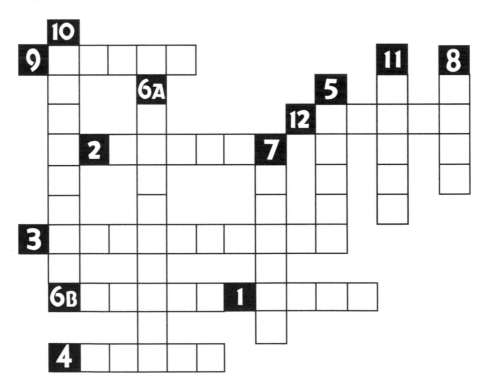

1. **(Across)** Matthew 28:1 WHAT time of day was it?

    _____

2. **(Across)** Matthew 28:1 WHAT day of the week was it?

    _____

    Here comes our special effect. Watch out!

3. **(Across)** Matthew 28:2 WHAT takes place?
    A severe _____

4. **(Across)** Matthew 28:2 WHO descends from heaven?
    An _____ of the Lord

    We need props.

5. **(Down)** Matthew 28:2 WHAT did he roll away?
    The_____

    Makeup and costumes please, A.K.

6. Matthew 28:3 WHAT did He look like?
    a. **(Down)** Appearance like _____
    b. **(Across)** Clothing as _____ as snow.

    Extras, we need you.

7. **(Down)** Matthew 28:4 WHO shook? The _____

8. **(Down)** Matthew 28:4 The guards shook in WHAT
    emotion? For _____ of him (the angel)

9. **(Across)** Matthew 28:6 WHAT has happened to Jesus?
    He has _____.

10. **(Down)** Matthew 28:11 WHAT did the guards do?
    They went into the city and _____ to the
    chief priests all that had happened.

11. **(Down)** Matthew 28:12 WHAT did the elders give the
    soldiers? A large sum of _____

12.   **(Across)** Matthew 28:13 WHAT did the elders want the
      soldiers to say?

      That the disciples came by night and _____
      Him while the soldiers were asleep.

      Matthew 28:15 Did the soldiers take the money?
      ____ Yes   ____ No

   Cut! What a scene. Those were some great special effects!
Were you surprised that the guards ran to report to the chief
priests and elders? How about the money the elders gave the
guards to lie?
   So if things don't go your way, you should lie, right? No
way! But that's exactly what the chief priests and elders did.
They couldn't stop
Jesus from coming
back no matter how
many guards they
posted or how heavy
the stone was because
nothing is impossible
with God! And since they
didn't get their way, they
decided to lie to keep
other people from
knowing the truth
that Jesus was the
Son of God. Did they succeed? ____ Yes   ____ No

   Tell WHY you think that on the lines below.

   _____

   _____

   _____

Now don't forget to run your lines before you go.

ACTION AT THE TOMB

It's great to have you back on the set. As we set up our scene for today's shoot in John, be sure to note how the scene begins. Is it the same day and the same time as the scene that we shot yesterday in Matthew? To find out, turn to John 20 on page 137 and help our script clerk make sure that these two scenes fit together. Read John 20:1-18.

"Now…places, everybody! The excitement is about to begin. We'll open with camera 3 on the tomb, so quiet down. Roll those cameras, and action!"

John 20:1 WHO came to the tomb?

_____

WHAT day and time was it when she came to the tomb?

_____

Is it the same day and time that we saw in Matthew?
_____ Yes   _____ No

WHAT had already happened when Mary arrived at the tomb?
The _____ was already taken from the _____.

John 20:2 WHO were the first two people that Mary ran to?

_____

WHAT did she tell them?

_____

_____

John 20:3-4 WHO gets to the tomb first? Do you know who the other disciple is—the one whom Jesus loved? Unscramble his name.
(oJnh)   ____   ____   ____   ____

John 20:5-7 WHAT did John and Peter see in the tomb?

_____

John 20:9 WHAT did John and Peter not understand?

_____

John 20:11-13 WHO was weeping and WHY was she weeping?

_____

_____

John 20:14-17 WHOM does Mary see?

_____

John 20:18 WHOM does Mary tell that she has seen the Lord?

_____

And *cut!* That was some great camera work. You captured Mary's distress, Peter and John's excited race to the tomb, and Mary's joy as she recognizes her living Lord!

DAY 5

CAST CHANGE

Wow! What an action-packed week it has been. As we prepare to shoot this last scene, our time is short. We need to make sure we capture the most important moments in our script. Let's start by doing a background check to find the key words in our script. Turn to pages 139-140 and read John 20:19-31, and then mark the following key words:

see / seen   believe / believed (you could
                                       color it blue)

Thomas

Now don't forget to mark anything that tells you WHEN. Do it with a clock like this:

Our assistant director would like for us to take a quick scan of our master script on Luke before we begin the shoot. Luke gives us a few more details than John does after Peter leaves the tomb. So read Luke 24:12-34, and then we'll be ready to begin.

"Is our cast ready to go? Good—then places, everyone." As we shoot this scene, fill in the blanks (including the blank with the box around it) with the correct answer. Then take each letter that is in a box and place it on the lines at the bottom to spell out a very important message that our moviegoers need to know.

1. Luke 24:13-15 WHO appears to the two on the road to Emmaus? ☐ __ __ __ __

2. Luke 24:30-31 HOW did they recognize Jesus? Their eyes were opened when Jesus broke the __ __ ☐ __ __.

3. Luke 24:33 After Jesus vanishes, WHO do the two go tell? The e __ __ __ __ __ d __ ☐ __ __ __ __ __ __ and those who were with them.

    Now back to our script on John 20.

4. John 20:19 Were the doors open or shut where the disciples were? __ ☐ __ __

5. John 20:19 WHAT time of day is it, and WHAT day is it? E __ __ __ __ __ __ on the f __ __ ☐ __ day of the week.

6. John 20:19 WHAT does Jesus say? "__ __ __ __ __ be __ __ __ ☐ y__ __."

7. John 20:19 WHY does Jesus say this? WHY are the doors shut? WHAT emotion were the disciples feeling? The disciples felt __ __ ☐ __ of the __ __ __ __.

8. John 20:20 WHAT does He show the disciples?
   His __ __ __ __ ☐ and His __ __ __ __

9. John 20:20 HOW do the disciples feel now that they've seen the Lord?
   They ☐ __ __ __ __ __ __ __.

10. John 20:24 WHO is not with the disciples when Jesus comes? __ __ __ __ __ __ called
    ☐ __ __ __ __ __ __

11. John 20:25 Thomas tells the disciples WHAT will make him believe.
    "Unless I ☐ __ __ in His __ __ __ __ __ the
    __ __ __ __ __ __ __ of the __ __ __ __ __,
    and __ __ __ my __ __ __ __ __ __ into the
    place of the __ __ __ __ __, and __ __ __
    my hand into His __ __ __ __, I will not
    __ __ __ __ __ __ __."

12. John 20:26 HOW many days was it before Jesus appeared again in their midst?
    After ☐ __ __ __ __ days

13. John 20:27-29 WHY does Thomas believe?
    Jesus said to him, "Because you have __ __ __ ☐ Me."

Now take all the letters in the boxes and place them in order on the lines below and find out the reason we celebrate Easter.

__ __ __ __ __   __ __ __
1   2   3   4   5   6   7   8

__ __ __ __ __!
9   10   11   12   13

As Jesus delivers His last line in verse 29, the director is ready for you. This is your moment. As the camera zooms in for a close-up, look straight into the camera and deliver the famous lines that tell us why John wrote this book. Here we go! The director is giving you your cue. John 20:31 and action!

Wow! That was great. Now that we've filmed Jesus' resurrection, why don't you gather your family or friends and act it out with them? You're sure to deliver a great performance, and just think how much fun you'll have reliving the most spectacular moment in all of history!

Before you leave the set, let's look at the evidence that proves that it really happened. We need to be able to tell other people how we know what we believe is the truth. Below are two false statements that people say to discredit the resurrection. Read the false statement, then look up the verse under the statement that shows us why this statement is false.

False: Christ did not really die. He swooned and was revived in the tomb.

Truth: John 19:32-34 First the soldiers saw WHAT?

_____

Then one of the soldiers _____ His side with

a spear, and immediately _____ and _____ came out.

Truth: John 19:39-40 They bound Jesus in

_____ _____ with about a

_____ pounds of spices.

Do you think the Roman soldiers made a mistake when they said Jesus was dead? Could you breathe wrapped up in linen with a hundred pounds of spices?
____ Yes ____ No

False: Christ was not really raised from the dead. The disciples were either hallucinating or having visions.

Truth: John 20:18 WHO saw the Lord? _____

Luke 24:13-16,31 WHO did Jesus appear to on the road to Emmaus? The ___ ___ ___

John 20:19-20 WHO rejoiced when they saw the Lord?

_____

John 20:26-28 Which disciple touched Jesus? _____

1 Corinthians 15:3-8 To WHOM did Jesus appear in verse 6? _____

at one time

So did all these people hallucinate? Have you ever seen 500 people hallucinating at one time? And why would the disciples steal the body, lie about it, and then lay down their lives spreading the good news about Jesus? Why would they give up their life for a lie? And most importantly, we also know that God's Word tells us that Jesus did rise again, and we know God's Word is the truth!

Isn't that AWESOME? Jesus didn't stay dead. He is alive, and one day soon He will come back for you and me!

So let's celebrate! Our sorrow has turned into joy! The cast and crew want to have a party. Let's help them out by making something to eat that will also remind us about why we're celebrating.

Ask your mom or a grown–up to help you make these great Resurrection Rolls.

RESURRECTION ROLLS

You'll need:

- large marshmallows—represents Jesus' body

- melted butter—represents the oils used in anointing the dead body

- 1/2 cup of sugar mixed with 1 teaspoon of cinnamon—represents the spices used to wrap Jesus' body

- can of crescent rolls—represents the linen wrappings that Jesus was wrapped in

1. Open the can of crescent rolls (your linen wrappings), and separate the dough into triangles.

2. Dip and roll one marshmallow (Jesus' body) into the melted butter (our anointing oil).

3. Roll the marshmallow into the cinnamon/sugar mixture (the spices).

4. Place the marshmallow in the center of the crescent triangle. Fold the roll over the marshmallow and pinch the edges tight. Put each crescent-wrapped marshmallow on a greased cookie sheet.

5. Bake the rolls as directed on the package. The oven represents the sealed tomb.

Once these are baked (our burial), we will find all that remains in the tomb is the linen wrappings (our crescent roll). The marshmallow is gone because Jesus has risen from the dead!

Now before you eat these great rolls, make sure you thank Jesus for coming to earth, suffering, and dying a criminal's death so that we can be resurrected with Him and have eternal life!

IT'S A WRAP!

Well, you did it! You shot the most amazing and stunning scene in all of history—the scene of the empty tomb. Our moviegoers are sure to gasp as they experience the earthquake, meet the stunning angels, watch Peter and John race to the tomb, witness Mary's sorrow as it turns into joy, and see the disciples' fear change to rejoicing! Hallelujah! Jesus is the resurrected King!

6

THE FINAL SHOOT

JOHN 21

Well, it's hard to believe that this will be our last week on the set. It sure has been exciting, and you have done such a wonderful job each week from running cameras, to gathering props, to helping with the makeup—and even standing in for Jesus!

As John closes this book, he has achieved his purpose. He has shown us over and over again who Jesus is and why these things were written. Now, in the last chapter, John has a very special message for us. Let's discover his message as we film the final moments in our movie.

SCAN THE SCRIPT!

Are you ready to create the last set of storyboards for our movie? If so, grab your colored pencils and your script for John 21. Don't forget the most important thing: Pray before you begin. We want those storyboards to give our director a clear idea of how to shoot this final scene.

Now that you're ready, turn to page 140 and read John 21. Draw your storyboard and title each scene.

John 21:1-14   John 21:15-25

_____ _____

_____ _____

WHERE: _____ WHERE: _____

Very artistic! The director is sure to love them. Now don't forget your new lines for the week. Check your script and write your new lines on a cue card, then practice those lines how many times today? _____ times

---

NOW SHOWING!

So when they had finished breakfast, Jesus said to Simon Peter,

"Simon, son of John, do you love Me more than these?" He said to Him, "Yes, Lord; You know that I love You." He said to him, "Tend My lambs."

—John 21:15

ON LOCATION

It's time to go on location once again. The director would like you to go with the assistant director to scout out this new location. Find out WHERE it is. WHAT props will we need? After you have decided WHERE this important scene takes place, help A.K. out as she gets Jesus and the rest of our cast ready for today's shoot. You'll need your script, so turn to pages 140-141 and read John 21:1-14. Don't forget to double-underline in green the <u>WHERE</u> that you find.

Now WHAT happens in John 21:1?

_____

WHERE is our location?

_____

WHO is on location with us? Unscramble the following names:
    a. mnsio etper _____ _____
    b. hotams _____
    c. ahantlane _____
    d. onss fo ebzedee _____ _____ _____
    (Who are these two? aseJm _____ and
    noJh _____—Mark 14:33)
    e. wto theors _____ _____

This is the third time that Jesus has appeared to His disciples since He was resurrected. The assistant director wants to take a time-out to make sure we have each one of our location scenes nailed down. Use the maze below that the art director has created. Start at the cross where Jesus died, and go to each location where the resurrected Jesus appeared to arrive at our present location.

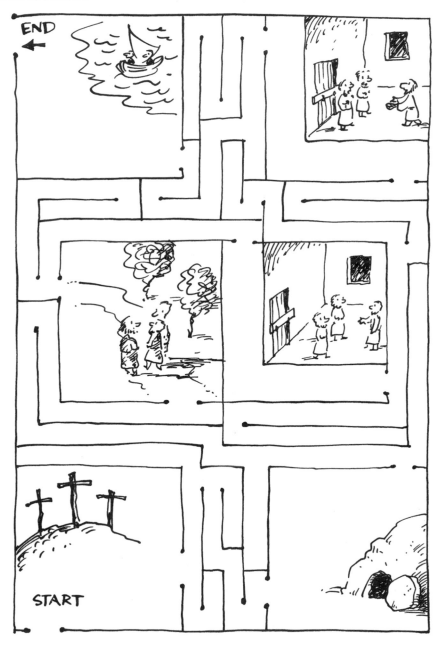

Good, we are right on target! Now that we are at our location, are our cast and crew ready to go? Besides Jesus, Peter will have the most important role today. This is a very important moment for Jesus and the impulsive Peter. So make sure Peter is ready, and then let's roll those cameras!

John 21:3 As our scene opens up, WHAT does Peter tell the others? "I am _____ _____."

John 21:3 Do the disciples go with Peter?
_____ Yes _____ No

Do they catch anything? _____ Yes _____ No

John 21:4-5 While they are in the boat, WHO calls to them?

_____

WHERE is He? On the _____

John 21:6 WHAT does Jesus tell them?

_____

Do they catch anything? _____ Yes _____ No

John 21:7 WHO recognizes Jesus?

_____

WHO throws on his clothes, jumps out of the boat, and swims to Jesus?

_____

John 21:9 WHAT do the disciples see when they get on land?

_____

John 21:10 WHAT does Jesus tell them to do?

_____

John 21:12 Jesus asks them to do WHAT?

_____

Cut! That was great, especially how you captured our impulsive Peter diving into the ocean to get to Jesus. Tomorrow we will see what happens after breakfast with Jesus. See you then.

MARK THE SCENE!

Before we continue filming our scene with Jesus and Peter, we need you to mark your script. This is so you will know what is important in our scene. Turn to pages 141-143 to John 21. Read John 21:14-25 and mark the following key words:

love (a red heart)　　　　　　　sheep (lambs)

follow

Now don't forget to rehearse your lines as you leave the set. Do you see any key words in your lines this week? Mark them on your cue card to help you as you practice these lines.

BACKGROUND CHECK

Now that we have discovered what is important in this scene by marking our key words, we are going to do a quick background check. We need to compare the things that Peter said and did before Jesus was crucified to things that are unfolding on our set today.

This comparison will help us understand why John put this final scene with Peter and the disciples in his book.

Read Luke 5:4-11 WHAT was Peter doing in these verses when Jesus called him to follow Him? WHAT was Peter's job?

_____

John 21:3-4 Now compare. WHAT is Peter doing when Jesus shows up?

_____

Read John 18:15-27.

John 18:18 WHERE is Peter when he denies Jesus?
By a c_____ f_____ warming himself

HOW many times does Peter deny Jesus? _____ times

John 21:9 Now compare. WHAT are the fish laid on?

_____

John 21:15-17 WHAT does Jesus ask Peter?

_____

HOW many times? _____

Read John 13:36-38.

WHAT did Peter tell Jesus he would do in verse 37?

_____

Did Peter succeed or did he fail?

_____

WHAT did he do three times?

_____

Peter failed. Instead of laying down his life for Jesus, he denied Him three times. When Jesus appears to Peter on the beach, He has something very important to show Peter. Jesus begins by reminding Peter of two things:

By showing up while Peter is fishing, Jesus is reminding Peter of how He called him to catch men instead of fish. He is reminding Peter of his calling.

Jesus builds a charcoal fire, which is sure to remind Peter of how he failed. Peter had denied Jesus three times while warming himself at a charcoal fire.

Is Jesus finished with Peter since Peter has failed Jesus by denying Him? _____ Yes _____ No

HOW can we know? Look at what Jesus says to Peter. Jesus asks him three times, "Do you love Me?" Then each time He gives Peter an instruction.

WHAT are the three instructions Jesus gives Peter in John 21:15-17?

verse 15: "_____ _____ _____."

verse 16: "_____ _____ _____."

verse 17: "_____ _____ _____."

Jesus is showing Peter His compassion, mercy, and forgiveness by affirming him three times in front of his friends. Peter had failed Jesus by denying Him three times, and now Jesus in His love and mercy affirms Peter three times. He is restoring Peter in front of the other disciples.

After restoring Peter, Jesus tells him what He wants him to do. Jesus tells Peter to take care of the sheep. Now who are the sheep? Do you remember how Jesus compared us to sheep in Isaiah 53:6? And in John 10:11 Jesus says He is the good shepherd who lays down His life for the sheep. Jesus is commissioning Peter to take the good news of the gospel to other people and to feed them with His Word. This shows us that Jesus isn't finished with Peter. Peter failed, but God still has a plan for his life.

Now how does this apply to you? This isn't just another scene on the beach. This scene reminds us how God reaches down and picks us up whenever we stumble and fall. Just like Jesus didn't abandon Peter when he stumbled, Jesus will not abandon you when you mess up. When we fail, we need to go to Jesus and tell Him we are sorry. We need to confess our sin to Him. And then, just like with Peter, Jesus will restore our relationship with Him.

As you leave the set today, think if there has been a time when you have failed to stand up for Jesus. If there has, go to Jesus and tell Him how sorry you are and ask Him to forgive you. Then thank Him for being merciful and kind, for giving you another chance to love and serve Him just like Peter!

FOLLOW ME!

You did a great job behind the scenes yesterday comparing the two events in Peter's life so that we can make sure our audience understands the importance of Jesus' discussion with Peter on the beach.

As we begin filming this scene today, finish up your investigation by reading John 21:18-25 on pages 142-143.

John 21:19 WHAT does Jesus tell Peter is going to happen to him in this verse? Peter is going to d ___ ___.

Would Peter's death glorify God? ____ Yes ____ No

WHAT did Jesus tell Peter to do?
"F ___ ___ ___ ___ ___   M ___!"

Remember how in John 13:37 Peter says he will lay his life down for Jesus? Now we see Jesus telling Peter that while he failed the first time to lay his life down for Him, he will glorify God in the end by laying his life down for Jesus.

John 21:20-21 WHAT does Peter ask Jesus about John in verse 21?

_____

Jesus has just told Peter how he is going to die, and that he is to follow Him. What is Peter's response? "But what about him?" (He was saying, "What about John?") Does that sound familiar? When your mom or dad asks you to do something, do you sometimes ask, "But, Mom, what about my brother or my sister? Why can't they do it?" _____ Yes _____ No

Let's look at Jesus' response.

John 21:22 WHAT does Jesus say?
"If I want him to _____ until I come,

_____ _____ _____ _____

_____? You _____ _____!"

Jesus is telling Peter, "Now listen, Peter, don't worry about John. I'll take care of John. You follow me!" So how does that apply to you? Should you be watching your friends to see what they are doing? And if they don't do what they should do or what Jesus told you to do, should that stop you from obeying Jesus?

_____

When your mom or dad tells you to do something, should you question them about your brother or sister, or just obey them by doing what they've told you to do?

_____

Jesus had a mission for Peter, and He wanted Peter's eyes on Him and not on what the other disciples would be doing. As we wrap up this scene, we can apply Peter's lessons to our life.

- Do you love Jesus? _____

- Have you put Him first in your life? _____

- Is your focus on Him and what He wants you to do, and not on what everybody else is doing?

- My focus is on _____

- Have you decided to follow Him? _____

Remember, the sheep are not just Peter's business. If you are a Christian, Jesus has given you special gifts and abilities. The sheep are your business, too. You can feed and tend Jesus' sheep by telling other people about Jesus and how to have eternal life, and by getting them to do these "Discover 4 Yourself" Bible Studies with you so that they can know truth for themselves. Serve Jesus by using the special gifts that He has given you.

Now as our movie draws to a close, say your lines. Pretend Jesus is talking to you. Tell Him how much you love Him, and then show Him by following Him!

iT'S A WRAP!

As we wrap up our final scene, let's take a look at John's final words in John 21:24-25. John is telling us that these words are true, and that he could have written many other things that Jesus did in his book, but that the world itself would not contain it all. Why did John choose to write what he did? So that we would see that Jesus is the Christ, the Son of God, and that believing we might have life in His name. John wants the world to know who Jesus is and what He did. That's why we made this movie—so the world can see Jesus.

We can also see why John included this last scene in his book. It's a scene that shows us the compassion of Jesus and how much He loves us. Even though we may fail Him, He never fails us! He has a purpose for each one of us to fulfill, and all we need to do is follow Him.

So the final scene is shot, and now an invitation is given. Do you believe? Have you given your life to Jesus? Will you follow Him?

Jesus is waiting. He is standing at the edge of heaven reaching out to you saying, "Look how much I love you. Do you love Me?"

The invitation has arrived. Will you accept it?

It's a wrap!

FiLM SpLiciNG!

Oops! Our director just found some bad places in the film we shot for our movie. The good news is that we have some film we can splice in to fix it. We need your help to replace this bad film by playing the game on page 116. You can play this game by yourself or you can ask your family or friends to play with you. One to four people can play. These are the things you will need to play:

- game board (page 116)
- cut-out filmstrip squares (page 117)
- coins or buttons for player tokens
- a coin to toss
- questions on pages 118-121

Instructions:

1. First cut out the filmstrip squares on page 117. Cut each square individually. You should have 24 squares.

2. Choose player tokens to mark your spot. More than one token may occupy the same square.

3. Mix the cut-up filmstrip squares and place them face-down on the table.

4. Before the game begins, each player receives several filmstrip squares, depending on how many people are playing the game. If there are one to two players, each player chooses four filmstrip squares. If there are three to four players, each player chooses two filmstrip squares.

5. Choose a player to begin. Let the youngest player go first.

6. To play the game, locate the questions on pages 118-121. Let one of the other players ask the question. If you

answer the question correctly, then flip the coin to see how many spaces you can move (heads moves two spaces, tails moves one space). You must answer the question correctly in order to flip the coin and move your token.

7. When a player moves, if he lands on a space with an X, he picks up a filmstrip square. The X spaces are the bad pieces of film in our movie that we need you to replace by completing the phrases on the board with the matching filmstrip squares. Once a player has picked up a new filmstrip square, if he can complete a phrase by laying down one or more of his filmstrip squares, he lays down those filmstrip squares and may move three extra spaces immediately on that turn. If he cannot lay down a complete phrase, he must choose one of his filmstrip squares to lay down on one of the phrases. It is then the next player's turn.

    Whenever any player lays down a filmstrip square that would allow you or someone else to complete a phrase, you must wait until you land on an X before you can lay down your matching pieces and move the three spaces.

    So don't forget to pick up a filmstrip square when you land on the X to replace the bad film with a good piece from your filmstrip squares.

8. If you land on an X and there are no more filmstrip squares left to pick up, you must still lay one of yours down if you have any left.

9. The player to reach the finish square first is the winner.

10. You need to reach the finish square by the exact number. If you have landed on the second to last spot you must flip heads to reach the finish square, or if you are only one space away you need to flip tails.

Now splice that film and have fun!

A NOTE FROM THE CAST AND CREW

You did it! You have finished the finale to our movie about Jesus. We are so proud of you and all your hard work! The movie has been edited and you are invited to the premiere showing. We want you to stand up and take a bow as the final credits roll. After all, we couldn't have done it without you!

Our prayer is that this movie will change the life of everyone who sees it. We know our lives were changed by experiencing firsthand what Jesus did for you and me! What agonizing heartbreak as we watched Jesus spend His final hours praying for us, being arrested, beaten, spit on, and mocked—and He lovingly submitted to it all. Jesus had a choice; He was and is God. He could have stopped it all with a word to His Father, but He chose to die so that you and I might live. And then, the most exciting part—the earthshaking earthquake and the empty tomb! Jesus did not stay dead. He was resurrected!

You have learned so much: how to find context, how to mark key words, and how to ask the 5 W's and an H! We want to send you a special certificate for all your hard work. Just fill out the card in the back of this book and mail it to us. Then keep looking up. Remember, Jesus is coming back one day soon to take us to heaven to live with Him. Now that would make an incredible movie! So as we say good-bye, remember Jesus—TO ETERNITY AND BEYOND! See you then!

The cast and crew

P.S. Now that you have completed our movies about Jesus' life (*Jesus in the Spotlight, Jesus—Awesome Power, Awesome Love,* and *Jesus—To Eternity and Beyond!*), we have some other adventures for you in God's Word. You might want to help Max, Molly, and Sam hunt down clues and become an inductive

Bible detective in *How to Study Your Bible for Kids.* Or maybe you would you like to be an investigative reporter. Get the scoop on Jonah in our study called *Wrong Way, Jonah!* You can help kids solve their problems by studying the book of James in *Boy, Have I Got Problems!* Then you can catch up with Max, Molly, and Sam once again as they help their Uncle Jake out on an archaeological dig in *God's Amazing Creation,* a study on the first part of Genesis. Whatever you choose, just remember how important it is for you to discover truth for yourself so that you can have a relationship with God!

GAME BOARD

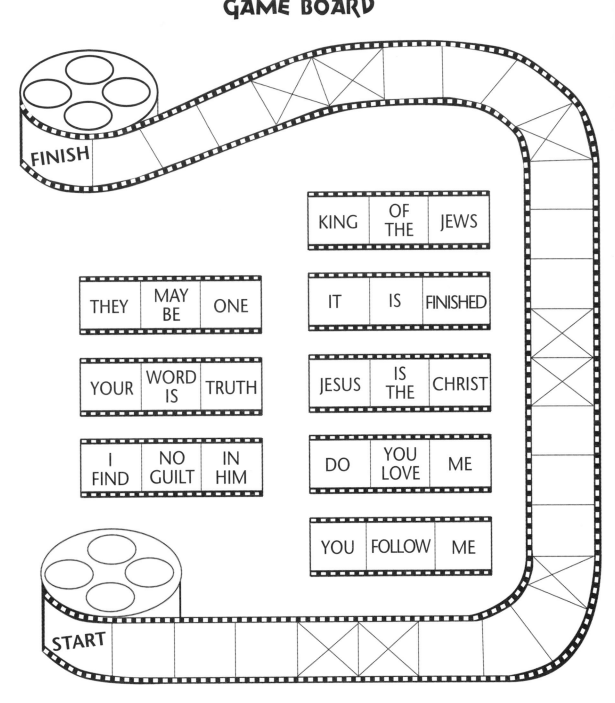

FINISH

KING | OF THE | JEWS

THEY | MAY BE | ONE

IT | IS | FINISHED

YOUR | WORD IS | TRUTH

JESUS | IS THE | CHRIST

I FIND | NO GUILT | IN HIM

DO | YOU LOVE | ME

YOU | FOLLOW | ME

START

FILMSTRIP SQUARES TO CUT OUT

KING	OF THE	JEWS

THEY	MAY BE	ONE

IT	IS	FINISHED

YOUR	WORD IS	TRUTH

JESUS	IS THE	CHRIST

I FIND	NO GUILT	IN HIM

DO	YOU LOVE	ME

YOU	FOLLOW	ME

GAME QUESTIONS

(Answers on page 124-126)

1. John 17 is about Jesus' p_____ to the Father.

2. John 17:1 WHAT does Jesus ask God to do?
   a. to let this cup pass from Him
   b. to take Him back to heaven
   c. to glorify His Son

3. What is eternal life, according to John 17:3?
   a. to be a good person　　　b. to go to church
   c. to know the only true God, and Jesus Christ

4. John 17:4 True or False: Jesus accomplished the work that God gave Him to do.

5. True or False: Jesus is praying for Himself, the disciples, and the world in John 17.

6. John 17:11 True or False: The two things that Jesus prays for His disciples are that God will keep them in His name, and that they may be one.

7. John 17:14 True or False: The world loves Jesus and the disciples.

8. John 17:15 True or False: Jesus wants the disciples kept from the world.

9. John 17:17 Jesus' request is for the disciples to be s_____ in truth.

10. John 18:1 Jesus and His disciples leave the upper room and go WHERE?

11. John 18:5 WHO betrays Jesus?

12. John 18:10 WHO cuts off the high priest's slave's ear?

13. John 18:13 True or False: Jesus is taken to Pilate first.

14. John 18:15 WHO follows Jesus?
    a. Judas　　b. Philip　　c. Peter

15. John 18:17-27 WHAT does Peter do before the rooster crows?
    a. falls asleep waiting to see what will happen to Jesus
    b. denies Jesus three times
    c. hides because he is afraid

16. John 18:22 True or False: The officer treats Jesus with respect.

17. John 18:24 WHERE does Annas send Jesus?
    a. Caiaphas   b. Pilate   c. Herod

18. John 18:28 True or False: The Jews do not enter the Praetorium because they do not want to defile themselves.

19. John 18:31 WHAT did Pilate tell the Jews to do with Jesus?
    a. Go home   b. Judge Him according to your law
    c. Take him to Herod

20. John 18:38 WHAT did Pilate tell the Jews?
    a. I find no guilt in Him.   b. Crucify Him.

21. Luke 23:7 True or False: Pilate sends Jesus to Herod.

22. Luke 23:11 True or False: Herod sends Jesus back to Pilate.

23. John 18:39 WHO does Pilate offer to release?
    a. Barabbas   b. the King of the Jews

24. John 18:40 WHOM does the crowd want?
    a. Barabbas   b. Jesus

25. John 19:1 True or False: Pilate has Jesus scourged.

26. John 19:2-3 WHAT three things do Pilate's soldiers do to Jesus?

    Twist together a _____ of thorns

    Put a purple _____ on Him

    Give Him _____ in the face

27. John 19:7 True or False: The Jews wanted to put Jesus to death because He made Himself out to be the Son of God.

28. John 19:19 True or False: The inscription Pilate wrote and put on the cross said: "Jesus the Nazarene, the King of the Jews."

29. John 19:23-24 WHAT did the soldiers do when they crucified Jesus?
    a. They sold His garments and clothing.
    b. They fought over His garments and sold His clothing.
    c. They divided His garments and cast lots for His clothing.

30. John 19:25-26 True or False: Mary (Jesus' mother), Mary the wife of Clopas, Mary Magdalene, and John witnessed Jesus' death.

31. John 19:30 WHAT did Jesus say before He died?

32. John 19:38 WHO was Joseph of Arimathea?
    a. a soldier   b. a secret disciple of Jesus
    c. the chief priest

33. John 19:39 True or False: Nicodemus brought 1000 pounds of myrrh and aloes.

34. John 19:42 WHY did they choose a nearby tomb?
    a. Because it was in a garden
    b. Because it was Jesus' family tomb
    c. Because the tomb was close by and it was the day of preparation

35. John 20:1 WHO came to the tomb early, on the first day of the week?
    a. Mary Magdalene
    b. Joseph
    c. Nicodemus

36. John 20:1 True or False: Mary saw the angel roll the stone away.

37. John 20:2 WHO were the first two people that Mary ran to?
    a. Peter and John
    b. John and James
    c. Peter and James

38. True or False: Mary told Peter and John, "The Lord has risen."

39. John 20:3-4 WHO gets to the tomb first?
    a. Peter   b. John   c. James

40. John 20:18 WHO does Mary tell that she has seen the Lord?
    a. Joseph and Nicodemus   b. the disciples

41. John 20:19 Were the doors open or shut where the disciples were?

42. John 20:19 WHEN Jesus finds the disciples, how are they feeling?
    a. They are rejoicing.   b. They are afraid.
    c. They are sad.

43. John 20:24 WHO is not with the disciples when Jesus comes?

44. John 20:27-29 WHAT makes Thomas believe?

45. John 21:3 True or False: Peter is fishing when Jesus appears on the beach.

46. John 21:7 WHO recognizes Jesus?

47. John 21:7 WHO throws on his clothes, jumps out of the boat, and swims to Jesus?

48. John 21:15-17 True or False: Jesus asks Peter, "Do you love Me?"

49. HOW many times did Jesus ask this question?

50. WHAT instruction does Jesus give Peter?
    a. Shepherd My sheep.
    b. Go back to fishing.

PUZZLE ANSWERS

Page 8

"But these have been written so that you may believe that Jesus is the Christ, the Son of God; and that believing you may have life in His name."

John 20:31

Page 51

Page 62

"I find no guilt in Him."

Pages 71-72

1. c		7. a	
2. f		8. c	
3. d		9. b	
4. a		10. a	
5. e		11. c	
6. f.			

Page 75

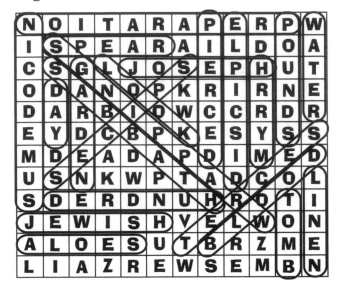

Page 82

"But these have been written so that you may believe that Jesus is the Christ, the Son of God; and that believing you may have life in His name."

—John 20:31

Page 86

Page 93
Jesus has risen!

Page 102

Answers to game questions on pages 118-119
1. prayer
2. c. glorify His Son
3. c. to know the only true God, and Jesus Christ
4. True
5. False. Jesus is praying for Himself, the disciples, and all believers—*not* for the world.
6. True

7. False. The world hates Jesus and the disciples.
8. False. Jesus wants the disciple, kept from the evil one, *not* from the world.
9. sanctified
10. garden of Gethsemane
11. Judas
12. Peter
13. False. Jesus is taken to Annas first.
14. c. Peter
15. b. denies Jesus three times
16. False. The officer strikes Jesus.
17. a. Caiaphas
18. True
19. b. Judge Him according to your law.
20. a. I find no guilt in Him.
21. True
22. True
23. b. the King of the Jews
24. a. Barabbas
25. True
26. crown of thorns, purple robe, give Him slaps in the face
27. True
28. True
29. c. They divided his garments and cast lots for His clothing.
30. True
31. "It is finished!"
32. b. a secret disciple of Jesus
33. False. It was 100 pounds, *not* 1000 pounds.
34. c. because the tomb was close by and it was the day of preparation
35. a. Mary Magdalene
36. False. The stone was already rolled away.
37. a. Peter and John
38. False. Mary said they have taken away the Lord out of the tomb, and we do not know where they have laid Him.
39. b. John

40. b. the disciples
41. shut
42. b. They are afraid
43. Thomas
44. Seeing Jesus, seeing His hands, and touching His side
45. True
46. John, the disciple whom Jesus loved
47. Peter
48. True
49. three
50. a. Shepherd My sheep.

OBSERVATION WORKSHEETS
JOHN 17-21

Chapter 17

1   Jesus spoke these things; and lifting up His eyes to heaven, He said, "Father, the hour has come; glorify Your Son, that the Son may glorify You,

2   even as You gave Him authority over all flesh, that to all whom You have given Him, He may give eternal life.

3   "This is eternal life, that they may know You, the only true God, and Jesus Christ whom You have sent.

4   "I glorified You on the earth, having accomplished the work which You have given Me to do.

5   "Now, Father, glorify Me together with Yourself, with the glory which I had with You before the world was.

6   "I have manifested Your name to the men whom You gave Me out of the world; they were Yours and You gave them to Me, and they have kept Your word.

7   "Now they have come to know that everything You have given Me is from You;

8   for the words which You gave Me I have given to them; and they received *them* and truly understood that I came forth from You, and they believed that You sent Me.

9   "I ask on their behalf; I do not ask on behalf of the world, but of those whom You have given Me; for they are Yours;

10 and all things that are Mine are Yours, and Yours are Mine; and I have been glorified in them.

11 "I am no longer in the world; and *yet* they themselves are in the world, and I come to You. Holy Father, keep them in Your name, *the name* which You have given Me, that they may be one even as We *are.*

12 "While I was with them, I was keeping them in Your name which You have given Me; and I guarded them and not one of them perished but the son of perdition, so that the Scripture would be fulfilled.

13 "But now I come to You; and these things I speak in the world so that they may have My joy made full in themselves.

14 "I have given them Your word; and the world has hated them, because they are not of the world, even as I am not of the world.

15 "I do not ask You to take them out of the world, but to keep them from the evil *one.*

16 "They are not of the world, even as I am not of the world.

17 "Sanctify them in the truth; Your word is truth.

18 "As You sent Me into the world, I also have sent them into the world.

19 "For their sakes I sanctify Myself, that they themselves also may be sanctified in truth.

20 "I do not ask on behalf of these alone, but for those also who believe in Me through their word;

21 that they may all be one; even as You, Father, *are* in Me and I in You, that they also may be in Us, so that the world may believe that You sent Me.

22 "The glory which You have given Me I have given to them, that they may be one, just as We are one;

23 I in them and You in Me, that they may be perfected in unity, so that the world may know that You sent Me, and loved them, even as You have loved Me.

24 "Father, I desire that they also, whom You have given Me, be with Me where I am, so that they may see My glory which You have given Me, for You loved Me before the foundation of the world.

25 "O righteous Father, although the world has not known You, yet I have known You; and these have known that You sent Me;

26 and I have made Your name known to them, and will make it known, so that the love with which You loved Me may be in them, and I in them."

Chapter 18

1 When Jesus had spoken these words, He went forth with His disciples over the ravine of the Kidron, where there was a garden, in which He entered with His disciples.

2 Now Judas also, who was betraying Him, knew the place, for Jesus had often met there with His disciples.

3 Judas then, having received the *Roman* cohort and officers from the chief priests and the Pharisees, came there with lanterns and torches and weapons.

4 So Jesus, knowing all the things that were coming upon Him, went forth and said to them, "Whom do you seek?"

5   They answered Him, "Jesus the Nazarene." He said to them, "I am *He*." And Judas also, who was betraying Him, was standing with them.

6   So when He said to them, "I am *He*," they drew back and fell to the ground.

7   Therefore He again asked them, "ᵃWhom do you seek?" And they said, "Jesus the Nazarene."

8   Jesus answered, "I told you that I am *He*; so if you seek Me, let these go their way,"

9   to fulfill the word which He spoke, "Of those whom You have given Me I lost not one."

10   Simon Peter then, having a sword, drew it and struck the high priest's slave, and cut off his right ear; and the slave's name was Malchus.

11   So Jesus said to Peter, "Put the sword into the sheath; the cup which the Father has given Me, shall I not drink it?"

12   So the *Roman* cohort and the commander and the officers of the Jews, arrested Jesus and bound Him,

13   and led Him to Annas first; for he was father-in-law of Caiaphas, who was high priest that year.

14   Now Caiaphas was the one who had advised the Jews that it was expedient for one man to die on behalf of the people.

15   Simon Peter was following Jesus, and *so was* another disciple. Now that disciple was known to the high priest, and entered with Jesus into the court of the high priest,

16 but Peter was standing at the door outside. So the other disciple, who was known to the high priest, went out and spoke to the doorkeeper, and brought Peter in.

17 Then the slave-girl who kept the door said to Peter, "You are not also *one* of this man's disciples, are you?" He said, "I am not."

18 Now the slaves and the officers were standing *there*, having made a charcoal fire, for it was cold and they were warming themselves; and Peter was also with them, standing and warming himself.

19 The high priest then questioned Jesus about His disciples, and about His teaching.

20 Jesus answered him, "I have spoken openly to the world; I always taught in synagogues and in the temple, where all the Jews come together; and I spoke nothing in secret.

21 "Why do you question Me? Question those who have heard what I spoke to them; they know what I said."

22 When He had said this, one of the officers standing nearby struck Jesus, saying, "Is that the way You answer the high priest?"

23 Jesus answered him, "If I have spoken wrongly, testify of the wrong; but if rightly, why do you strike Me?"

24 So Annas sent Him bound to Caiaphas the high priest.

25 Now Simon Peter was standing and warming himself. So they said to him, "You are not also *one* of His disciples, are you?" He denied *it*, and said, "I am not."

26 One of the slaves of the high priest, being a relative of the one whose ear Peter cut off, said, "Did I not see you in the garden with Him?"

27 Peter then denied *it* again, and immediately a rooster crowed.

28 Then they led Jesus from Caiaphas into the Praetorium, and it was early; and they themselves did not enter into the Praetorium so that they would not be defiled, but might eat the Passover.

29 Therefore Pilate went out to them and said, "What accusation do you bring against this Man?"

30 They answered and said to him, "If this Man were not an evildoer, we would not have delivered Him to you."

31 So Pilate said to them, "Take Him yourselves, and judge Him according to your law." The Jews said to him, "We are not permitted to put anyone to death,"

32 to fulfill the word of Jesus which He spoke, signifying by what kind of death He was about to die.

33 Therefore Pilate entered again into the Praetorium, and summoned Jesus and said to Him, "Are You the King of the Jews?"

34 Jesus answered, "Are you saying this on your own initiative, or did others tell you about Me?"

35 Pilate answered, "I am not a Jew, am I? Your own nation and the chief priests delivered You to me; what have You done?"

36 Jesus answered, "My kingdom is not of this world. If My kingdom were of this world, then My servants would be fighting so that I would not be handed over to the Jews; but as it is, My kingdom is not of this realm."

37 Therefore Pilate said to Him, "So You are a king?" Jesus answered, "You say *correctly* that I am a king. For this I have been born, and for this I have come into the world, to testify to the truth. Everyone who is of the truth hears My voice."

38 Pilate said to Him, "What is truth?" And when he had said this, he went out again to the Jews and said to them, "I find no guilt in Him.

39 "But you have a custom that I release someone for you at the Passover; do you wish then that I release for you the King of the Jews?"

40 So they cried out again, saying, "Not this Man, but Barabbas." Now Barabbas was a robber.

Chapter 19

1   Pilate then took Jesus and scourged Him.

2   And the soldiers twisted together a crown of thorns and put it on His head, and put a purple robe on Him;

3   and they *began* to come up to Him and say, "Hail, King of the Jews!" and to give Him slaps *in the face.*

4   Pilate came out again and said to them, "Behold, I am bringing Him out to you so that you may know that I find no guilt in Him."

5   Jesus then came out, wearing the crown of thorns and the purple robe. *Pilate* said to them, "Behold, the Man!"

6   So when the chief priests and the officers saw Him, they cried out saying, "Crucify, crucify!" Pilate said to them, "Take Him yourselves and crucify Him, for I find no guilt in Him."

7   The Jews answered him, "We have a law, and by that law He ought to die because He made Himself out *to be* the Son of God."

8   Therefore when Pilate heard this statement, he was *even* more afraid;

9   and he entered into the Praetorium again and said to Jesus, "Where are You from?" But Jesus gave him no answer.

10 So Pilate said to Him, "You do not speak to me? Do You not know that I have authority to release You, and I have authority to crucify You?"

11 Jesus answered, "You would have no authority over Me, unless it had been given you from above; for this reason he who delivered Me to you has *the* greater sin."

12 As a result of this Pilate made efforts to release Him, but the Jews cried out saying, "If you release this Man, you are no friend of Caesar; everyone who makes himself out *to be* a king opposes Caesar."

13 Therefore when Pilate heard these words, he brought Jesus out, and sat down on the judgment seat at a place called The Pavement, but in Hebrew, Gabbatha.

14 Now it was the day of preparation for the Passover; it was about the sixth hour. And he said to the Jews, "Behold, your King!"

15 So they cried out, "Away with *Him*, away with *Him*, crucify Him!" Pilate said to them, "Shall I crucify your King?" The chief priests answered, "We have no king but Caesar."

16 So he then handed Him over to them to be crucified.

17 They took Jesus, therefore, and He went out, bearing His own cross, to the place called the Place of a Skull, which is called in Hebrew, Golgotha.

18 There they crucified Him, and with Him two other men, one on either side, and Jesus in between.

19 Pilate also wrote an inscription and put it on the cross. It was written, "JESUS THE NAZARENE, THE KING OF THE JEWS."

20 Therefore many of the Jews read this inscription, for the place where Jesus was crucified was near the city; and it was written in Hebrew, Latin *and* in Greek.

21 So the chief priests of the Jews were saying to Pilate, "Do not write, 'The King of the Jews'; but that He said, 'I am King of the Jews.'"

22 Pilate answered, "What I have written I have written."

23 Then the soldiers, when they had crucified Jesus, took His outer garments and made four parts, a part to every soldier and *also* the tunic; now the tunic was seamless, woven in one piece.

24 So they said to one another, "Let us not tear it, but cast lots for it, *to decide* whose it shall be"; *this was* to fulfill the Scripture: "THEY DIVIDED MY OUTER GARMENTS AMONG THEM, AND FOR MY CLOTHING THEY CAST LOTS."

25 Therefore the soldiers did these things. But standing by the cross of Jesus were His mother, and His mother's sister, Mary the *wife* of Clopas, and Mary Magdalene.

26 When Jesus then saw His mother, and the disciple whom He loved standing nearby, He said to His mother, "Woman, behold, your son!"

27 Then He said to the disciple, "Behold, your mother!" From that hour the disciple took her into his own *household.*

28 After this, Jesus, knowing that all things had already been accomplished, to fulfill the Scripture, said, "I am thirsty."

29 A jar full of sour wine was standing there; so they put a sponge full of the sour wine upon *a branch of* hyssop and brought it up to His mouth.

30 Therefore when Jesus had received the sour wine, He said, "It is finished!" And He bowed His head and gave up His spirit.

31 Then the Jews, because it was the day of preparation, so that the bodies would not remain on the cross on the Sabbath (for that Sabbath was a high day), asked Pilate that their legs might be broken, and *that* they might be taken away.

32 So the soldiers came, and broke the legs of the first man and of the other who was crucified with Him;

33 but coming to Jesus, when they saw that He was already dead, they did not break His legs.

34 But one of the soldiers pierced His side with a spear, and immediately blood and water came out.

35 And he who has seen has testified, and his testimony is true; and he knows that he is telling the truth, so that you also may believe.

36 For these things came to pass to fulfill the Scripture, "NOT A BONE OF HIM SHALL BE BROKEN."

37 And again another Scripture says, "THEY SHALL LOOK ON HIM WHOM THEY PIERCED."

38 After these things Joseph of Arimathea, being a disciple of Jesus, but a secret *one* for fear of the Jews, asked Pilate that he might take away the body

of Jesus; and Pilate granted permission. So he came and took away His body.

39 Nicodemus, who had first come to Him by night, also came, bringing a mixture of myrrh and aloes, about a hundred pounds *weight.*

40 So they took the body of Jesus and bound it in linen wrappings with the spices, as is the burial custom of the Jews.

41 Now in the place where He was crucified there was a garden, and in the garden a new tomb in which no one had yet been laid.

42 Therefore because of the Jewish day of preparation, since the tomb was nearby, they laid Jesus there.

Chapter 20

1 Now on the first *day* of the week Mary Magdalene came early to the tomb, while it was still dark, and saw the stone *already* taken away from the tomb.

2 So she ran and came to Simon Peter and to the other disciple whom Jesus loved, and said to them, "They have taken away the Lord out of the tomb, and we do not know where they have laid Him."

3 So Peter and the other disciple went forth, and they were going to the tomb.

4 The two were running together; and the other disciple ran ahead faster than Peter and came to the tomb first;

5 and stooping and looking in, he saw the linen wrappings lying *there;* but he did not go in.

6   And so Simon Peter also came, following him, and entered the tomb; and he saw the linen wrappings lying *there*,

7   and the face-cloth which had been on His head, not lying with the linen wrappings, but rolled up in a place by itself.

8   So the other disciple who had first come to the tomb then also entered, and he saw and believed.

9   For as yet they did not understand the Scripture, that He must rise again from the dead.

10   So the disciples went away again to their own homes.

11   But Mary was standing outside the tomb weeping; and so, as she wept, she stooped and looked into the tomb;

12   and she saw two angels in white sitting, one at the head and one at the feet, where the body of Jesus had been lying.

13   And they said to her, "Woman, why are you weeping?" She said to them, "Because they have taken away my Lord, and I do not know where they have laid Him."

14   When she had said this, she turned around and saw Jesus standing *there*, and did not know that it was Jesus.

15   Jesus said to her, "Woman, why are you weeping? Whom are you seeking?" Supposing Him to be the gardener, she said to Him, "Sir, if you have carried Him away, tell me where you have laid Him, and I will take Him away."

16   Jesus said to her, "Mary!" She turned and said to Him in Hebrew,

"Rabboni!" (which means, Teacher).

17 Jesus said to her, "Stop clinging to Me, for I have not yet ascended to the Father; but go to My brethren and say to them, 'I ascend to My Father and your Father, and My God and your God.'"

18 Mary Magdalene came, announcing to the disciples, "I have seen the Lord," and *that* He had said these things to her.

19 So when it was evening on that day, the first *day* of the week, and when the doors were shut where the disciples were, for fear of the Jews, Jesus came and stood in their midst and said to them, "Peace *be* with you."

20 And when He had said this, He showed them both His hands and His side. The disciples then rejoiced when they saw the Lord.

21 So Jesus said to them again, "Peace *be* with you; as the Father has sent Me, I also send you."

22 And when He had said this, He breathed on them and said to them, "Receive the Holy Spirit.

23 "If you forgive the sins of any, *their sins* have been forgiven them; if you retain the *sins* of any, they have been retained."

24 But Thomas, one of the twelve, called Didymus, was not with them when Jesus came.

25 So the other disciples were saying to him, "We have seen the Lord!" But he said to them, "Unless I see in His hands the imprint of the nails, and put my finger into the place of the nails, and put my hand into His side, I will not believe."

26 After eight days His disciples were again inside, and Thomas with them. Jesus came, the doors having been shut, and stood in their midst and said, "Peace *be* with you."

27 Then He said to Thomas, "Reach here with your finger, and see My hands; and reach here your hand and put it into My side; and do not be unbelieving, but believing."

28 Thomas answered and said to Him, "My Lord and my God!"

29 Jesus said to him, "Because you have seen Me, have you believed? Blessed *are* they who did not see, and *yet* believed."

30 Therefore many other signs Jesus also performed in the presence of the disciples, which are not written in this book;

31 but these have been written so that you may believe that Jesus is the Christ, the Son of God; and that believing you may have life in His name.

Chapter 21

1 After these things Jesus manifested Himself again to the disciples at the Sea of Tiberias, and He manifested *Himself* in this way.

2 Simon Peter, and Thomas called Didymus, and Nathanael of Cana in Galilee, and the *sons* of Zebedee, and two others of His disciples were together.

3 Simon Peter said to them, "I am going fishing." They said to him, "We will also come with you." They went out and got into the boat; and that night they caught nothing.

4 But when the day was now breaking, Jesus stood on the beach; yet the disciples did not know that it was Jesus.

5 So Jesus said to them, "Children, you do not have any fish, do you?" They answered Him, "No."

6 And He said to them, "Cast the net on the right-hand side of the boat and you will find *a catch*." So they cast, and then they were not able to haul it in because of the great number of fish.

7 Therefore that disciple whom Jesus loved said to Peter, "It is the Lord." So when Simon Peter heard that it was the Lord, he put his outer garment on (for he was stripped *for work)*, and threw himself into the sea.

8 But the other disciples came in the little boat, for they were not far from the land, but about one hundred yards away, dragging the net *full* of fish.

9 So when they got out on the land, they saw a charcoal fire *already* laid and fish placed on it, and bread.

10 Jesus said to them, "Bring some of the fish which you have now caught."

11 Simon Peter went up and drew the net to land, full of large fish, a hundred and fifty-three; and although there were so many, the net was not torn.

12 Jesus said to them, "Come *and* have breakfast." None of the disciples ventured to question Him, "Who are You?" knowing that it was the Lord.

13 Jesus came and took the bread and gave *it* to them, and the fish likewise.

14 This is now the third time that Jesus was manifested to the disciples, after He was raised from the dead.

15 So when they had finished breakfast, Jesus said to Simon Peter, "Simon, *son* of John, do you love Me more than these?" He said to Him, "Yes, Lord; You know that I love You." He said to him, "Tend My lambs."

16 He said to him again a second time, "Simon, *son* of John, do you love Me?" He said to Him, "Yes, Lord; You know that I love You." He said to him, "Shepherd My sheep."

17 He said to him the third time, "Simon, *son* of John, do you love Me? Peter was grieved because He said to him the third time, "Do you love Me?" And he said to Him, "Lord, You know all things; You know that I love You." Jesus said to him, "Tend My sheep.

18 "Truly, truly, I say to you, when you were younger, you used to gird yourself and walk wherever you wished; but when you grow old, you will stretch out your hands and someone else will gird you, and bring you where you do not wish to *go*."

19 Now this He said, signifying by what kind of death he would glorify God. And when He had spoken this, He said to him, "Follow Me!"

20 Peter, turning around, saw the disciple whom Jesus loved following *them*; the one who also had leaned back on His bosom at the supper and said, "Lord, who is the one who betrays You?"

21 So Peter seeing him said to Jesus, "Lord, and what about this man?"

22 Jesus said to him, "If I want him to remain until I come, what *is that* to you? You follow Me!"

23 Therefore this saying went out among the brethren that that disciple

would not die; yet Jesus did not say to him that he would not die, but *only*, "If I want him to remain until I come, what *is that* to you?"

24 This is the disciple who is testifying to these things and wrote these things, and we know that his testimony is true.

25 And there are also many other things which Jesus did, which if they were written in detail, I suppose that even the world itself would not contain the books that would be written.

DISCOVER 4 YOURSELF!

INDUCTIVE BIBLE STUDIES FOR KIDS

Bible study can be fun! Now kids can learn how to inductively study the Bible to discover for themselves what it says. Each book combines serious Bible study with memorable games, puzzles, and activities that reinforce biblical truth. Divided into short lessons, each individual study includes:

- a weekly memory verse
- Bible knowledge activities—puzzles, games, and discovery activities
- Optional crafts and projects to help kids practice what they've learned

Any young person who works through these studies will emerge with a richer appreciation for the Word of God and a deeper understanding of God's love and care.

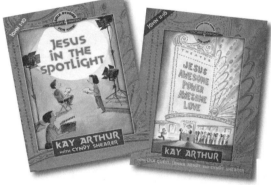

Kay Arthur and Cyndy Shearer
Kids "make" a movie to discover who Jesus is and His impact on their lives. Activities and 15-minute lessons make this study of John 1–10 great for all ages!
ISBN 0-7369-0119-1

Kay Arthur, Janna Arndt, Lisa Guest, and Cyndy Sh[...]
This book picks up where *Jes[...] the Spotlight* leaves off: [...] 11–16. Kids join a movie te[...] bring the life of Jesus to th[...] screen in order to learn key t[...] about prayer, heaven, and Jesus.
ISBN 0-7369-0144-2

Kay Arthur and Janna Arndt
As "advice columnists," kids delve into the book of James to discover—and learn how to apply—the best answers for a variety of problems.
ISBN 0-7369-0148-5

Kay Arthur and Janna Arndt
This easy-to-use Bible study combines serious commitment to God's Word with illustrations and activities that reinforce biblical truth.
ISBN 0-7369-0362-3

Kay Arthur and Janna Arndt
Focusing on John 17–21, children become "directors" who must discover the details of Jesus' life to make a great movie. They also learn how to get the most out of reading their Bibles.
ISBN 0-7369-0546-4

Kay Arthur and Scoti Domeij
As "reporters," kids investigate Jonah's story and conduct interviews. Using puzzles and activities, these lessons highlight God's loving care and the importance of obedience.
ISBN 0-7369-0203-1

Kay Arthur and Janna Arndt
God's Amazing Creation covers Genesis 1–2-those awesome days when God created the stars, the world, the sea, the animals, and the very first people. Young explorers will go on an archaeological dig to discover truths for themselves!
ISBN 0-7369-014[...]